The letter of Paul to the

ROMANS

Christian Life—the Beginning *and* Progress,
with Concept-to-Concept Commentary

M. C. Paul

WESTBOW
PRESS®
A DIVISION OF THOMAS NELSON
& ZONDERVAN

WestBow Press books may be ordered through booksellers or by contacting:

WestBow Press
A Division of Thomas Nelson & Zondervan
1663 Liberty Drive
Bloomington, IN 47403
www.westbowpress.com
1 (866) 928-1240

ISBN: 978-1-4908-8674-9 (sc)
ISBN: 978-1-4908-8675-6 (e)

Library of Congress Control Number: 2015910287

Print information available on the last page.

WestBow Press rev. date: 07/15/2015

Contents

Acknowledgements

In April 1969, at the age of 21, I committed my life to Jesus Christ in an Evangelistic meeting of Dr. Akbar Abdul Haqq, associate evangelist of Dr. Billy Graham. I acknowledge with gratitude, the contribution of these men of God, in my turning to Him. I began grappling with the truth concerning Law and Grace quite early. It was only after I had studied the epistle of Romans, I understood what all happened to me when I had committed my life that day. I came to know that I was justified by faith. I praise the Lord for the ministry of Rev. Dr. John R. W. Stott. His books inspired me to devote my time for further study of Romans. The few lectures I heard from him, the brief time I spent with him and the correspondence that followed these helped me to love expository study and preaching. Now, I am learning more and more to be subjected to the Law of the Spirit of Life in Christ Jesus to overcome the Law of Sin and Death.

I thank all my good friends who have been advising me to write a commentary on Romans. It is only a year after the publication of my first book 'Being Tossed To and Fro? The Way to Steady Yourself!', the Lord has given me the strength to undertake the present work. I thank my fellow believers Mr. Sunil Potharaju, Mr. Maruthi Paul Kumbham, Mr. Rama Rao Mahanthi and Mr. Kishore Chintha for typing the material. My thanks are due to Rev. Thomas Thomas, Birmingham, UK, a friend of our family for his patient reading of the manuscript and for his invaluable words of appreciation. I thank my younger son John Stephen for making the work to take its present form. My thanks are due to my elder son Paul Isaac for his support. My wife Suguna prompts me to depend on the Lord in all situations. My daughter Tabitha Agnes encourages me to be focused on the ministry. The families of my three children are with them in their support. The extended families of my brothers and sisters always stand by me in my spiritual endeavours. I thank all of them. I would like to thank Kathy Lester, Kayla Stobaugh, Adam Tinsley and all the staff of the WestBow Press, a division of Thomas Nelson for their valuable publishing and distribution services. Thank you.

M. C. Paul

Email: paulcmgm@yahoo.co.in
Mobile: +91-9440039270
Address: #21-244/1, Noble Colony
Machilipatnam – 521001
Andhra Pradesh, India

Introduction (1:1 - 15)

Most people in the world long for establishing contact with God. Christians claim that they have found the way for having not mere contact with God but a relationship with Him as well. They say that this relationship is through the new life in Jesus Christ, with God as the Father. This life has a beginning and it has to progress from day to day. Does Paul, the author of the epistle of Romans, want both the Jews and the Gentiles in the world to know this? We may have to say 'yes', if we consider the progress of his presentation in the epistle. This may be the idea behind writing such a long letter to the Church in Rome, a Church which he never visited hitherto. First, he wanted them to know what all happened to them when they believed. He knew that they were all saved men and women who began to live this new life. He made it clear to them that they live this new life because they were justified by God when they put their faith in Christ. Secondly, he wanted them to know the possibility of leading a victorious life.

Paul has so many good words about the members of the Church in Rome. We are not sure who founded the Church. Circumstances those days, point to a possibility that it was founded by the converted Hellenistic Jews, who returned from Jerusalem after their experience of Pentecost. He knew the strategic importance of the Church. It was a fast growing Church located in the capital city. He placed before them the teaching he consolidated during his first two missionary journeys. No wonder, his presentation is very near to systematic theology! But we know that his concern was the life in Christ which is to be enjoyed by the members of the Church there and everywhere. So far as the date of writing this epistle is concerned, there is every reason to believe that this epistle was written between 57 and 59 AD. The probable place of writing is Corinth.

The theme of the epistle, 'justification by faith', is not Paul's afterthought in his ministry. It is seen in his very first message in the synagogue at Pisidian Antioch during his first missionary journey. He pointed out that they were not able to be justified by the Law and told them that it would happen only through faith in Jesus. (Ac. 13:39) Paul had known it by his own experience. God was merciful to Paul as his heart's desire, in his struggle with the Law, was to please God. Paul says, '... I was shown mercy because, I acted in ignorance and unbelief.' (I Ti. 1:13) In the Church history those who followed the Law with utmost sincerity like Paul went through such intense struggle. God was merciful to them too. They found victory when they understood the implications of the promise, 'the just shall live by faith'. St. Augustine in 4th century and Martin Luther in 16th century AD are good examples of those who found this life of victory through the epistle of Romans. Others who do not go through this intense struggle and yet say they follow the Law may remain as Pharisees and Scribes in Christianity. These people try to please God on their own terms.

There is an interesting point in Paul's claims about himself. Once he was constrained to present his credentials of his Orthodox Judaism by listing at length in the epistle to the Philippians. He claims that he is faultless so far as his legalistic righteousness is concerned. (Ph. 3: 5, 6) If we infer from the seventh chapter of Romans that the struggle is personally about himself, we can understand that for Paul, all that mattered was his relationship with God. The Law was unable to make him rightly relate himself with God. It only satisfied his ego. He was justified only by the grace of God through faith in the resurrected Lord. Later he struggled to please God in his new found relationship with Him, by keeping the Law. It was a futile attempt. Then the revelation he received helped him to opt for the Law of Spirit of life in Christ Jesus leaving out the Law of sin and death. Thus he found victory. He wants all the believers to avail this opportunity to live a life of Christian victory. In Paul's understanding the meaning of the phrase 'the just shall live by faith' can better be expressed this way: 'those who are set right with God shall live'. This life he calls as 'the life according to the Law of the Spirit of life in Christ Jesus'.

There are some who argue saying that the predominant theology of Paul is on the theme 'in Christ' and not on the theme 'justification by faith'. They say that the subjective mystery of 'in Christ' is central to Paul's theology and not the objective reality of 'justification by faith'. But in the epistle of Romans we notice that these two are present not only together but also in the right order. 'Justification by faith' is the entry point into Christ while 'in Christ' is the life which a believer lives, according to 'the Law of Spirit of life in Christ Jesus'. 'Justification by faith' is like jumping at the offer into the life-boat in the face of calamity, and 'in Christ' is like setting a sail safe to the shore.

Paul begins the epistle by greeting and relating himself (1:1 - 15)

The epistle begins with his usual way of writing. He never loses sight of his special calling as an Apostle. He sees his apostleship as the will of God. He leaves no room for speculation that the early twelve or any one among them commissioned him as an Apostle. He is conscious that he is writing to a Church he never visited and is making sure that they receive it, the way they should receive an epistle from anyone of the Apostles. He sees himself as the one set apart for the Gospel. He presents it as a no afterthought of God but as Gospel which was hidden all along the course of human history in the Holy Scriptures. As one among the Jews, he echoes the Jewish expectations of the Messiah. He says that the Gospel declares that in Jesus Christ those promises of the prophets are fulfilled. He says that the Gospel relates to His Son Jesus Christ who is a descendant of David so far as His human nature is concerned; God by raising Him from the dead declared with power that He is the Son of God through the Spirit of Holiness.

In Paul's view, grace of God, is the life-line for any human being. He sees himself as the recipient of it, to call people from Gentiles. Grace is undeserved favour that God shows to any person. He proceeds to declare the splendour of it which not only releases the guilty from the punishment for sin but also brings them into God's fold by adoption as sons of God. We can see God's grace this way: God sacrificed His Son on the cross for sinful men not just to leave them to live as unpunished men but to take them into His home as sons, to live the life of His Son. A true story is told of a believing Bishop in the remote past. He pleaded with the judge, who sentenced the assassin of his son to hanging, and got him released. The convict was pleasantly surprised and expected that the Bishop would ask him to leave from the court premises and never to show his face. But the Bishop took him to his house, opened the doors of the room of his son and pleaded with him to fill the place vacated by his son. He obliged in tears. The life of the adopted son subsequently reflected truly the life of the deceased son. This is a demonstration of God's grace in miniature.

The way Paul relates himself with people should mark him the greatest among the Apostles. Very few believers are known to him in the Church in Rome. Yet He keeps all others along with them in his heart and keeps thanking the Lord for their faith, which he says, is reported all over the world. We can notice from this that Paul sees the central place of the Church which God gave to them. We can very easily see why Paul wrote such an elaborate letter to them presenting the doctrine in an orderly manner. He believes that the Church in Rome with the help of transport and communication facilities, available to it, will surely spread the Gospel to the Gentiles everywhere. It can disseminate also his teaching to the Church at large. He expresses his desire to visit them with a hope to be sent by them to Spain, but he commits everything to the will of God.

Paul is at the height of his popularity at the time of writing this epistle. He is full of energy to back his zeal. Besides these, he is brimming with confidence in the grace of the Lord. Yet he is all the more humble in relating himself with the Roman Church. His desire, to see that he and the believers in the Church would be mutually strengthened by each other's faith, reveals his humility. This is the way a Church should be built. He teaches this at length in Corinthian and the Ephesian epistles. If all-sufficiency attitude is seen in the ministers these days, it needs correction.

Doctrinal Exposition (1:16 - 8:39)

Highlights the theme of the epistle (1:16, 17)

The theme 'justification by faith' is the dominant theme in this epistle. There are subthemes present in it. All these are expressed in word pictures. The following are the word pictures that he employs: 1. 'Justification by faith' brings the picture of a courtroom where a person is declared not guilty. 2. 'Redemption' brings the picture of a marketplace where a slave in those days was freed. 3. 'Reconciliation' presents the picture of a place where an estranged relationship is restored. 4. 'Propitiation' brings the picture of the temple where sacrifice is offered for forgiveness of sins. 5. 'Adoption' brings the picture of a home where documentation for sonship is made and 6. 'Reckoning' presents the picture of an accounting office where crediting the personal account of a person is done.

Paul chooses verse 4 of chapter 2 from the book of Habakkuk as the basis for his theme. Habakkuk first, complains to God about the perversion of justice in Israel. God says that He will raise up Babylonians to punish them. He describes how they execute His judgment. Habakkuk gets horrified at this and brings in his second complaint: why the Lord should allow the wicked to swallow up those who are more righteous than themselves. Then he waits for His answer on a watchtower. We see God's justice in its splendour in His reply to this. There is no division like wicked and more wicked, Israelites and the rest, in God's sight. It is only those who are justified by their faith will live. God does not show favouritism. (Ro. 2:11) God asks Habakkuk to note down the revelation on a tablet so that the proclaimer may run and proclaim it. It is such a brief proclamation that even busy people running around can also read and listen to it. This conveys the brevity, importance and urgency of the message.

This is the message which Paul calls as the Gospel. He says that it is a mystery made known to him by revelation. He states: "this mystery is that through the Gospel the Gentiles are heirs together with Israel, members together of one body and sharers together in the promise in Christ Jesus." (Eph. 3:6) This falls in line with the revelation given to Habakkuk. In which everyone is treated equal so far as God's justice is concerned. The revelation Paul received enabled him to elaborate on trusting in Jesus. (Jn. 14:1) Paul says, "... what I received I passed on to you as of first importance: that Christ died for our sins according to the Scriptures, that he was buried, that he was raised on the third day according to the Scriptures." (I Co. 15:3, 4) This gives us the clue as to what it is to trust in Jesus. It is trust in His death and resurrection, in the final analysis. Gospel is the power of God for the salvation of everyone who believes: first for the Jew, then for the Gentile. (V. 16) He says that the righteousness of God is revealed in the Gospel. This is to be obtained by faith. This is to be enjoyed throughout the lifetime of a believer. It is faith addressed to faith which is a march forward from faith to greater faith.

Proves that entire mankind is under God's wrath (1:18 - 3:20)

Begins with the Gentiles (1:18 - 32)

Paul begins his doctrinal exposition by taking up the case of Gentiles first. According to him the godless are those who see God's eternal power and His divine nature in creation and still refuse to honour Him and be thankful to Him. They fill their hearts with all sorts of things in the name of wisdom only to blur their sight. They refuse to acknowledge His presence lest they should become accountable to Him. They find an easy way of escaping His presence by making for themselves images. Equating God with anything which comes to the mind, however lofty the thought might be, is an insult to God. They reject general revelation given by God and want a god on their terms. They turn away from the immortal God only to fall into self-assertion and self-deception. They have right relationship neither with God nor with man. So they try to prove themselves by suppressing the truth about God. Paul calls this state of affairs of Gentiles, as godlessness and wickedness. He says that the wrath of God is on them.

Self-assertion and self-deception lead them to self-indulgence. Paul says that, God, because of all these gave them over to sinful desires, shameful lusts and to a depraved mind. How wretched man can become we can't even imagine. Paul describes at length the acts of a perverted man. When we see these in our society these days we wonder how things remain the same through the centuries. It is the result of exchanging truth of God for a lie and worshipping and serving created things rather than the creator. The special mentioning on abandoning natural relations by women to live with women and men to live with men presents the seriousness of sexual impurity those days. These days are no different from those. All other things he mentions are direct consequences of godlessness in the society. These are: "They have become filled with every kind of wickedness, evil, greed and depravity. They are full of envy, murder, strife, deceit and malice. They are gossips, slanderers, God-haters, insolent, arrogant and boastful; they invent ways of doing evil; they disobey their parents; they have no understanding, no fidelity, no love, no mercy. Although they know God's righteous decree that those who do such things deserve death, they not only continue to do these very things but also approve of those who practice them." (1:29-32). Paul proves that the Gentile community stands condemned before God.

Deals with those who claim to be different (2:1 - 16)

In the former days there were great moral teachers in the Greek world. During Paul's days their teachings were prevalent. The followers claimed themselves to be different in the decadent world. They believed themselves to be the guardians of moral life of the society. In so doing they became moralizers. It is true that they are not idol worshippers. They claimed themselves to be disapprovers of all kinds of immorality. In their sight they are promoters of virtue. When Paul addresses them straight, we can understand that he is targeting their judgmental capacity. This, in essence is the argument of Paul: when they judge others guilty while doing the same things themselves, don't they come under the judgment of the true judge who is just and fair and who is above man? Teachers who talk of 'do's and don't's' and 'right and wrong' fall into a trap. They end up only as sayers but not doers. Yet they continue delighting in their teaching covering up their immoral life. They end up as hypocrites. They presume that God is not watching them. They don't realize that He is tolerant and is rich in kindness. Instead of responding to Him in repentance they show a lenient attitude.

From 5th verse onwards we notice that Paul is proving that God is a righteous judge. His wrath is on all those who do not rightly relate themselves with Him and with one another. Their actions betray this failure to relate. Paul proceeds to present the nature of God's judgment. He calls His judgment as righteous judgment which will be revealed. He makes some universal statements applicable for all ages in human history. If these are rightly understood some of the questions of the curious men could be answered with ease. Paul says that, God will reward each person according to what he has done. God does not show favouritism. There is trouble and distress waiting for those who do evil and glory, honour and peace waiting for those who do good. This applies both to Jews and Gentiles. Paul categorises their actions into two. They are found in the seventh and eighth verses. All along human history there are men who respond to the level of revelation they receive from God. They persist in doing good, seeking glory, honour and immortality. They seek manifestation of God, His approval and the joy of being with Him forever. It is faith in the work of the one true God - faith, which is forward looking in the Old Testament days (Jn 8:56; Gal 3:8) or backward looking in the New Testament days, unknowingly, to the cross. It is only with such understanding we can consider the word 'eternal life' in verse 7. We need to carefully note that it applies only to those who died without hearing the Gospel. In contrast to it there are those who reject to surrender to the revelation they receive. They are self-seeking men who wilfully follow their evil ways with deliberate intention to suppress the truth. They always look to gratify themselves. Only wrath and anger of God awaits them.

In the light of verse 23 of chapter 3, any passage before it is to be understood. Paul is continuing his argument from verse 12 onwards. His argument revolves around moral values of Gentiles. He is comparing the conscience keeping Gentile with the Law keeping Jew, who has a higher revelation. He says that none of these two would escape punishment if sin is found in him. The same Law of God operates in the case of Gentiles and Jews. A Gentile is to act according to the Law written in his heart and the Jew is to act according the written Law he has with him. The Gentile acts, naturally, incurring either the approval or disapproval of his conscience. Paul states that those who do not just hear the Law but obey the Law are righteous in God's sight. And only they are declared righteous. By saying this he is underscoring the impossibility of keeping the conscience as God's Law. He says that it is not enough just to appreciate moral values and teach those. It will not ensure God's declaration of them as righteous.

Now, turns to Jews (2:17 - 3:20)

Paul to the Philippians, as a point for his argument, says, "though I myself have reasons for such confidence. If someone else thinks they have reasons to put confidence in the flesh, I have more: circumcised on the eighth day, of the people of Israel, of the tribe of Benjamin, a Hebrew of Hebrews; in regard to the law, a Pharisee; as for zeal, persecuting the church; as for righteousness based on the law, faultless." (Ph 3:4-6). He has the background to assess where a Jew really stands. Now, he knows that these did not help him to rightly relate himself with God. It is mere revelation, nothing else, that gave him conviction and courage to address the Jew straight. He knows the mind of a Jew and his deepest feeling in his heart. He presents his understanding of the feelings of a Jew on his privileges by listing the following matters: a Jew claims himself to be able to know the will of God and to be able to approve what is superior, because of his instruction in the Law; he presumes and claims himself to be a guide for the blind, a light to those who are in the dark, an instructor to the foolish and a teacher of infants. All these claims he makes because he is in possession of the Law which is an embodiment of knowledge and truth. Paul says that all these lead a Jew to brag about himself. Paul now questions his accountability and integrity in his personal life. Paul questions, "you, then, who teach others, do you not teach yourself? You who preach against stealing, do you steal? You who say that people should not commit adultery, do you commit adultery? You who abhor idols, do you rob temples? You who boast in the law, do you dishonor God by breaking the law?" (Vs. 21 to 23) He unearths the hidden life of a Jew. Then expresses his shock at the state of affairs, using an Old Testament statement: "God's name is blasphemed among the Gentiles because of you." (V. 24)

The idea of true circumcision as distinct from circumcision of only the flesh was present even in the days of Moses. (Dt. 10:16) Circumcision is a sign of the covenant of God with the people of Israel. They agreed to keep the Law when Moses put before them the promises of God. Then God made a covenant with them. Paul talks here at length about true circumcision. He says that if a Jew breaks the Law he would become as though he had not been circumcised. He comes from the other side and wants to know from him, whether the one who was not physically circumcised, but who keeps the Law, would not he be considered as circumcised. All his realistic questions put a Jew on the mat. Then he makes a strong statement which may offend any Jew. He says that anyone who is a Jew outwardly is not a Jew and any circumcision only physical is not a circumcision, unless it is an act involving the Spirit. God's delight is the test of it all!

From chapter 3 verse 1 onwards we see Paul talking about God's faithfulness which his readers may question. Paul is very well able to imagine how a Jew in his heart feels, after all the negative remarks he hears from Paul about the privileges of his birth and circumcision. Perhaps he has been encountering such offended Jews time and again. They definitely feel shocked. There is every reason for them to question Paul, asking him whether it was all futile for them to keep themselves separate as Jews, observing circumcision strictly all through the centuries. 'What privilege did it leave for them after enduring and persisting in this?', was their question. To this Paul says that it is advantageous in every way. The predominant privilege of being a Jew is that he is trusted with the word of God. Of course, there are some who did not have faith. That cannot nullify God's faithfulness. He expresses his strong desire to see God as true even if everyone is a liar. Now, he is able to visualize, that they would turn back and come forward with an argument as a corollary to his statement. He anticipates their argument: then why should God judge us if our unrighteousness enhances His righteousness? Is it not unjust on His part to bring wrath on us? He responds saying outright no to it. Though he is their fellow human being, Paul says that he is justified in saying outright no to it. He argues saying, 'since God is the Judge of the human beings, it is impossible for him to be unjust'. He anticipates their counter argument. The man says: if my falsehood is enhancing God's glory, why should God condemn me as a sinner? And in the same breath this man shouts aloud echoing others, who say, 'let us do evil that good may result'. Paul recoils at this and pronounces that they deserve their condemnation since they want to persist in this argument.

From 9th verse onwards, Paul, takes us to a courtroom situation where prosecution procedure is completed. He begins by saying that the privileges of the Jews make them, all the more, condemnable because, the greater the privilege the greater is the responsibility, to keep the Law. The higher the revelation the higher is the carefulness expected from them with regard to sin. Now he is able to make a sweeping statement that Jews and Gentiles alike are all under sin. He proceeds to list a number of references quoting from different books of the Old Testament to show the all-pervasiveness of sin in human life. They show that their thoughts and actions are under the power of sin. He lists the parts of the body - tongue and lips of the mouth; feet and hands; mind and eyes etc. - which are affected by the power of sin. (Vs. 9-18) The Law given as special revelation to the Jews and the conscience which is given in nature to the Gentiles make both of them equally accountable before God. They become speechless. One of the most important functions of the Law according to Paul is to make them become conscious of sin. Paul says that they only become conscious of sin and with the help of the Law, they can never hope to be declared justified in His sight. What insight this is, of a man who went close to the Lord after his encounter with Him!

Shows that faith is the way open for all (3:21 - 5:21)

Presents God's dealing of the situation (3:21 - 26)

The passage which is from verse 21 to verse 26 is the most important part in the doctrinal presentation of Paul. It presents compactly the entire dealing of God with regard to human sin and its punishment. The situation presented is that of a guilty sinner, standing before the judge, looking all around for help. This is the human predicament. In that dark situation, the sinner finds a ray of hope. That is the grace of God, the Judge! Grace is favour on the undeserved. But, how would God the just judge forgive a guilty sinner? It is a pertinent question in the light of the commandment of God that judges should acquit the innocent and condemn the guilty. (Dt. 25:1) Paul answers this question by mentioning about the fulfilment of the Old Testament hope of redemption. Everyone is in need of such redemption irrespective of who he is: a Jew or a Gentile; immoral or a moralizer etc. This includes everyone in the past, present and future, irrespective of his country, language complexion, race, caste or any other human categorization, because sin is universal. The universality of sin is presented by Paul in verse 23. It reads like this: "for all have sinned and fall short of the glory of God". In this verse God's glory can be understood as, His approval of man or man's entry into His presence or as the image and likeness of His son which he intended to see in man. Man missed this. Hence Paul says that he fell short of the glory of God. The meaning of sin could be seen here as missing the mark.

Days of fulfilment of Old Testament hope have arrived. God in His grace has acted. A righteousness of God apart from Law has been revealed. It comes to those who believe. It is through faith in Jesus Christ, His Son. It is God's offer of His relationship. It is not through works of the Law but through faith in Jesus Christ His Son. Paul attributes every aspect of the whole process to God. This is to be understood in the vocabulary, syntax and grammar, he employs. Righteousness is right relationship with God, which He gives to the guilty sinner by justifying him. Justification is a declaration. It is God who declares a guilty sinner, that he is not guilty. It is God telling the sinner: 'You are set free; You are acquitted'. The wonder of the declaration is the positive aspect of it. It is not asking him to leave the courtroom and never to show his face. Instead, it is asking him to come into His house to enjoy the height, length, width and depth of His grace.

Paul presents the fulfilment of Old Testament hope. God's act of redemption and propitiation is its fulfilment. Redemption is a word which is used in a market place. The slaves are set free with a price. This was to be the practice, if a slave is to be released into freedom. Paul sees the need for man to be freed from the tyrant, sin. A slave to sin is redeemed now by the payment of a price which is the precious blood of Jesus Christ. Paul lets these implications unfold subsequently in sixth, seventh and eighth chapters. The word 'propitiation' is an appropriate translation for the Greek word used here. The translation, 'expiation', suits in the sacrificial system of a temple. Here, the guilty sinner appeases an irate and hot tempered deity by an offer from his own possession. But in Paul's presentation, the provider of the offering is also God and His wrath is just, on a sinner. His Son is the sacrificial lamb who has voluntarily offered Himself on the altar. It is God's provision in which the Son gives Himself. The Son is none other than the second person in the Holy Trinity. It is now acceptable to God to blot away the sin of man. The subject and object of it all is God. This need not make us shy away from believing it, as the provider of animals in the Old Testament sacrificial ceremony was also God Himself. (Vs. 24 and 25 f)

In this act of propitiation, Paul says, God is demonstrating His justice, where He is proved to be just in justifying those who have faith in Jesus. He looked for a basis for His grace. It is the blood of the Cross. This brings into limelight His justice in this act of justification of the sinner. He is just. Paul says that we can say only Amen to it. So the source of justification is the grace of God and the ground of justification is the blood of His Son shed on the cross as sacrifice for sin. Justification is to be received through faith in the blood of His Son. The objective reality, which is an accomplished act on the Cross at a point of time in history, is to be received as a subjective reality in the present. It is through faith. Since it is a completed act of God there cannot be a human part in it. Hence it is to be received as a free gift. The means of receiving it is faith. So faith is not a merit. The merit a person hopes to acquire through good works will never enable him to set his relationship right with God. The righteousness of God is to be received, putting aside all efforts to earn merit in God's sight. Faith is telling God, 'I believe in the sacrificial death of your Son for my sins. I accept this offer of justification in faith. Thank you.'

Defends the universal role of faith (3:27 - 31)

If a man is justified by faith apart from observing the Law, it leaves no room for boasting at all. Works of the Law have no role in justification. Hence boasting of earning merit is not allowed. Paul is able to sense the deepest feeling of a Jew in his continual observance of the Law. In a particular context, he calls himself, a Hebrew of Hebrews, with regard to his race and blameless in observing the Law, with regard to his personal life. He is conscious of his undertone. He knows that there is every possibility for him to be tempted to boast. It is the problem of a human heart. Man wants to earn merit to please God - that too on his own terms. Paul finds fault with self-reliance of man - both before and after his salvation. (Eph. 2:8) He asks 'where then is boasting?'. And says that it is excluded on the principle of faith. After his conversion experience, he refuses to boast about anything excepting Christ and His Cross.

17

His next question concerns with the discrimination between a Jew and a Gentile. A Jew knows that he is of the chosen race - the seed of Abraham. He remembers the covenant God made with Abraham. He is conscious of the sign of the convent, the circumcision in his body. He claims for himself the blessing of God. In so doing, he forgets the second part of the promise God gave to Abraham and drifts into looking down on Gentiles. (Eph. 2:11, 12) Paul asks him to remember that God is one and so He is not only God of the Jews but also God of the Gentiles. It is amazing to see how he wants to bring them to their senses by his questioning. He is taking them beyond Abraham back to the origin of the human race, when from one man He made every nation of men. (Ac. 17:26). Paul proves himself to be a child of God truly emancipated. He raises himself above every human prejudice. In his argument he brings in the second part of the covenantal promise of God to Abraham which says that through his offspring all the nations of the earth will be blessed. (Ge. 22:18) The offspring is Jesus Christ. So, Paul concludes the present argument saying that God will justify the circumcised by faith and the uncircumcised through the same faith. Then Paul takes up the sensitive issue of the relationship between faith and Law. After all these arguments and counter arguments he brings them to a state where they realize that they are not nullifying the Law by this faith. In fact they are to realize that they are upholding the Law. How it is being done, he does not explain immediately. He deals with the role of the Law later while talking on Christian victory.

Takes support from the life of Abraham (4:1 - 25)

An average Jew is familiar with the Old Testament. The Rabbis and the Jewish sects are, all the more, familiar with it. Paul wants the Jewish and Gentile Christians to know that his teaching on 'justification by faith' is in line with the Scriptures. He takes the believing community to see the rich heritage they have. The seed of Abraham should know why Abraham is called as the friend of God. And should also know what it all means and why David is called as a man after God's own heart. They know that God calls Himself as God of Abraham, God of Isaac and God of Jacob, their Patriarchs. They also know that the Messiah would come from the lineage of David. They always boast of themselves as the ones belonging to these men of God.

Paul says that if Abraham was justified by works, there would be reason for him to boast about himself. But it was not so. He asks them to turn their Scriptures to see whether it talks about his work. He quotes verse 6 of Genesis 15. It reads: "Abraham believed the Lord and He credited it to him as righteousness". Paul, here, brings an ordinary situation to show that, wages a man earns for his work are not a gift but a reward for his labour. He says, "... now to the one who works, wages are not credited as a gift but as an obligation. However, to the one who does not work but trusts God who justifies the ungodly, their faith is credited as righteousness." (Ro. 4:4, 5) God credits righteousness in a man's account, who not only does not work but also is wicked in his life and conduct. It is only, that faith in such justifying God, which is reckoned as righteousness. What a bold expression of the depth of God's grace! Paul scores out the role of works in this. After this answer, Paul quotes verses 1 and 2 from Psalm 32 to make them see that David is saying the same thing. David is able to see the blessedness of a man whose sin, the Lord will never count against him. There is no reason why the Lord does it excepting for His grace. The only means for having this blessedness is by faith in His provision. Not by works!

19

Here, a special mention is needed on a controversy which many Bible scholars have been dealing with. It is this: Paul quotes Genesis 15 verse 6 to prove that justification is by faith and not by works. But, James mentions an event from Genesis 22, where God reiterates the covenant with Abraham, to prove that justification is not only by faith but also by works. Here appears a contradiction between Paul and James but it is only apparent. If we carefully look at the portions and the context in which they use the word faith, we notice that Paul is talking about the faith which is on the finished work of Christ for acceptance into God's family. This faith is determinative in character; it is measured as a single unit. But James is talking about the faith that should express itself in warm deeds of love. It is also faith on the finished work of Christ. The only difference is the continuing attitude of this faith in the believer. It can be measured in degrees. While Paul's focus is on the entry point of Christian life, James is concerned with the progress of that life. Paul is talking about the deposit of Christ's righteousness a person receives. James is talking about the righteousness that should come out in a person's everyday life. (Jas. 2:14-17)

After dealing with works, Paul takes up the topic of the place of circumcision in the scheme of things from 9th verse onwards. Paul wants them to know whether this blessedness is only for the circumcised or also for the uncircumcised. The way he questions them should naturally startle them. Their thinking would go to the very beginning of the rite of circumcision. He puts them another question to make them think whether Abraham's faith was credited to him as righteousness after he was circumcised or before. Then he proves again from the Scriptures that it was before but not after. God asks Abraham to undergo circumcision promising that it will be the sign of the covenant between God and him. (Ge. 17:11) Paul calls it a seal of the righteousness, that he received by faith while he had been still uncircumcised. He takes it as a proof for calling Abraham the father of those who have not been circumcised but only believed. He emphasizes the importance of the faith of Abraham before he was circumcised. The circumcised can also claim the fatherhood of Abraham, if they walk in the same faith. It is interesting to note his uncompromising attitude with regard to the subject of 'justification by faith'. It is not enough to be circumcised to call Abraham their father. They are to walk in the footsteps of Abraham who had that faith before he was circumcised. He proves from the Scriptures that justification is not by circumcision but by faith alone.

From 13th verse onwards he turns his attention to prove that justification is also not by Law. Abraham received the promise that he would be heir of the world. His offspring rejoice saying that Abraham is heir of the world and that they are children of Abraham. Paul says: 'yes it is true'. They might be entertaining some ideas. He is not bothered to answer whether it is true that they rule the world. We know that the seed of Abraham, the Messiah is the ruler. It is the kingdom community which inherits the earth. Paul is now concerned about proving that this inheritance is not by Law but by faith in the promise. By now they must have understood that justification is neither by works nor by circumcision. So it is easy for him to state that it is not by Law. It is very simple to understand. Law demands obedience but promise expects acceptance. Law is to be obeyed but promise is to be received. Abraham received the promise. If those who live by the Law are heirs, it amounts to saying that faith is of no value and promise is empty. If they want to live by the Law, they should know that there is transgression and this transgression provokes God's wrath. If there is no Law the topic of transgression does not arise at all. Hence promise which precedes the Law only gives hope. It is by faith and through the grace of God the promise is received by all of Abraham's offspring. These are people of the Law and also people of the faith of Abraham. So faith is the leveller of all. God appointed Abraham as the father of us all. We notice how Paul is rejoicing along with all those who are in the faith. This brings meaning to the name, Abraham as he is truly, the father of the nations.

Abraham believed in God who is not only the creator but also the sustainer of life. He created the universe out of nothing and life and death are in His hands. He gives life to the dead and calls things that are not as though they were. Abraham knew the one in whom he believed. The object of his faith was important to him. There are apparently degrees of faith as Paul talks of faith that can be weakened (V. 19) and faith that can be strengthened. (V. 20) Behind the promise he saw the power of God. He knew that the one who promised would fulfil His promise. So this is rational faith. His reasoning is based on his consideration of the power and character of the one who gave the promise. When God showed him the stars of the sky and told him, 'so shall your offspring be', Abram believed the Lord. (Ge. 15:5, 6) God changed his name to Abraham saying that He has made him father of many nations. (Ge. 17:5) Paul says that Abraham faced the fact that his body was as good as dead at about 100 years of age and that Sarah's womb was also dead. Yet he didn't allow his faith to be weakened. He persuaded himself to believe that God had power to carry out what he had promised. This faith was credited to him as righteousness. In so strengthening his faith, he gave glory to God. His readiness to offer Isaac is a clear example of his continuing attitude of faith. James talks about this in his epistle. (Jas. 2:23) His faith at the time of justification and the continuing attitude throughout is to be common for all believers. Paul says that the words 'it was credited to him' are written not only for Abraham but also for all those who believe. He includes in this list all those who believe in his time along with himself. He is identifying himself again with all those, who in future believe in God, who raised Jesus from the dead. He says that God handed him over to death for all their sins and raised Him from death for their Justification.

Lists the accompanied blessings (5:1 - 11)

Paul's language takes a definite turn to first person plural (we) and its pronoun (us). This very well fits to Paul whose convictions are unshaken so far as his solidarity with the believing community is concerned. He entreats everyone to enjoy himself the peace he has with God because of justification and reconciliation. This state of blessedness is only through Jesus Christ. It is for all those who believe. As those who believe, we have now, not only entered into God's grace but also stand in it. He says that we rejoice in our hope of the glory of God and also rejoice in the accompanied sufferings. He lists the progressive links of the chain which lead to hope in His glory: sufferings - perseverance - character - hope. This hope is on God who gave us the Holy Spirit by whom the love of God is poured into our hearts. Basing on this fact, Paul assures his readers that, this hope will not let them down.

When Paul says that God gave us the Holy Spirit, he does not speak of some special experience. He does not say that we have waited and received the Holy Spirit as a separate experience. The first disciples were filled by the Holy Spirit on the day of Pentecost. It took place at a definite point of time in the Bible. They were asked by the risen Lord to wait during that time when he was totally absent from them. If we examine the timescale, we notice that there were three stages for them. But, today, we have only two stages. We are either without Christ or with Christ. The

Gospel is all that which causes the difference and faith in Christ is the criterion to have Him in our hearts as the indwelling Spirit. It is the first statement of Paul in Romans about experiencing the Holy Spirit. He talks about the presence of the Holy Spirit in a believer. It is logical to think that Paul takes this experience as a natural result of justification a person receives. He talks about this experience in the same breath in which he talks about justification. For him, these two are inseparable. A person who is justified naturally has the Spirit of God. The love, the Holy Spirit lavishes in his heart is the love, from God which is to be enjoyed and shared. This is the love which God demonstrated for us in the death of his Son when we were still sinners.

Paul, now, is talking about the merits of the death and resurrection of God's Son and also about the benefits which accrue to a believer who is reconciled with God. He makes a mention of the power of the life in the risen Lord which is made available to the believer. This gives him confidence when he thinks of the wrath of God which will be revealed on the Final Day of Judgment. Paul reminds him about the, 'I am with you always' life of the Lord Jesus which sees him through. He uses the word salvation which has many facets - health, prosperity, victory over the enemy, forgiveness of sins etc. Of all these, forgiveness of sins is the key facet. If it is present everything else is also present along with it. (8:32) Paul employs the verb 'save' with different tenses to show different stages in the life of a believer. When he says that you are saved, he means that you are saved from the penalty of sin. (Eph. 2:8) When he says that we are being saved, he means that we are being saved every day from the power of sin (I Co. 1:18) and when he says that we shall be saved he means that we shall be saved from the presence of sin on the Day of Consummation. (Ro. 13:11) So the word 'salvation' can be expressed possessively, progressively and also prospectively. We are justified (no penalty), we live the life in the Spirit (no power of sin over us) and we will live the life on the other shore (no presence of sin).

Contrasts and compares sin and grace (5:12 - 21)

We rejoice in God because we are reconciled with Him through His Son Jesus Christ. So Paul wants to show the difference it made in our life because of the new fountainhead of humanity, Jesus Christ. Adam was created sinless. Jesus Christ was born sinless. Adam fell when he was tempted. Jesus Christ overcame temptation. Jesus Christ, now, is the fountainhead of the new humanity. Paul says that sin entered through one man and death through sin. He says that death came to all because all sinned. It is Adam who disobeyed the command of God. But death came to all till Moses though there was no Law till the time of Moses. Paul says that this happened in spite of the fact that sin need not be taken into account when there is no Law. We can infer from it that sin of Adam is inherited by all men. The writer to Hebrews argues that Levi offered tenth to Melchizedek. But he was not born. He was still in the body of Abraham. The writer considers it as though Levi offered it to Melchizedek when Abraham offered it. (Heb. 7:9) The same logic we can apply here, saying that, we too disobeyed the command of God, when Adam disobeyed, as we were all in his body. Besides this, we have already noted that the requirements of the Law are written on the hearts, and their conscience is the witness of their violation. (2:15) Hence Paul concludes saying that death came to all because all sinned.

The grace of the one man, Jesus Christ is overwhelming grace. Condemnation is because of only one sin of Adam but the gift followed many trespasses. This gift brought justification. Death reigned due to the trespass of one man. Paul contrasts its reign with the reign through Jesus Christ, of all those who receive God's abundant provision of grace in their life. The reign of these people is far above the reign of death. Paul now compares the results: the result of one trespass and the result of one act of righteousness. While the former brings condemnation, the latter brings justification, which is life for all men. The disobedience of one man made many sinners. When compared with it the result of the obedience of one man Jesus Christ is superior. This brings righteousness to many. The value of it is a continuing right relationship with God and the corollary of it is the possibility of continuing right relationship with man.

Paul says that death reigned from the time of Adam till the time of Moses, even though there was no Law. If that is so, there is nothing much to protest when Paul says, to their shock, that the Law was added so that the trespass might increase. (V. 20) Now he brings into picture the true ruler in the reign of death. Through death, sin which is universal, rules over all men. As sin reigns grace is to reign through righteousness. The result of the rule of sin is death while the result of the rule of grace is righteousness. It is the relationship with God which leads to eternal life. Eternal life is both physical and spiritual. Paul talks about the 'more than proportionate increase' of grace when compared to the increase of sin. Even while he is talking about it, he is conscious of the possibility of a wrong logical argument a man may resort to for his own detriment.

Talks of getting rid of sin's rule (6:1 - 14)

He takes up this wrong approach and deals with it. He can very well imagine how those who want to live a licentious life may respond to the doctrine of abundant grace. The Greek thought, of the body as evil and the spirit as good, can be at the back of their mind. One extreme position in such a thinking is to live a licentious life and hope for the release of the spirit. They love to do away with the Law. There are others who are thoroughly upset when Paul says that the Law was added that the trespasses might increase. Both the groups watch impatiently as Paul applies his doctrine to everyday practical life. The former are antinomians while the latter are legalists. In this situation his task should be to unsettle the antinomians and astonish the legalists - the former by counter argument and the latter by unfolding the implications of fulfilling the Law.

He begins it by questioning, 'shall we go on sinning so that grace may increase?' He quickly answers it by saying, 'by no means!' He puts a question which needs serious consideration by his readers that time and by all of us down the centuries. He says, 'we died to sin. How can we live in it any longer?' What does he mean when he says 'we died to sin'? He elaborates it. He equates baptism into Christ with baptism into His death. The burial with Jesus Christ through baptism is only to live a new life. This life can be experienced as Jesus Christ was raised through the glory of God. His question, 'don't you know?' should cause His readers to long for the experience of knowing what all that happened when they believed and were baptized. Paul is saying that they died to sin. So far as the death of Jesus Christ is concerned, it is both a representative death and also a substitutionary death. He died on our behalf and also in our place. Paul says, "The death he died, he died to sin once for all; but the life he lives, he lives to God." (V. 10) The death of Jesus to sin mentioned here is the penalty He bore on our behalf. When once the penalty is paid, we too can say that we died to sin and the case on us is closed. Paul's argument can be better understood this way: 'how can you open the case when it is closed?'. 'Dead to sin' according to Paul is 'dead to guilt'. You cannot recall guilt by sinning. Sin continues to lure us. But we can say no to it. We say that the penalty is paid. That is all we say to it.

The death of Jesus is unique. It is an event in history. But we can unite ourselves by faith with Him in His death by hoping to share in His life. If such is our unity with Him in His death, the natural result of it is our resurrection with Him. The old self or former life of a believer was crucified with Christ, so that his flesh which has been ruled by sin might be released from such rule. Death should naturally free a man from the bondage of sin. For a believer, this experience of knowing what all has happened in him is needed. The believer is a member of the body of Christ. So Paul, here, exhorts the readers to join him in believing that they will live with Him if they died with Him. This is only because Christ was raised from the dead and because death cannot touch Him again. The masterly grip of death over Him is once for all removed. The death He died, He died to sin once for all. The penalty of sin is fully paid. But so far as His life is concerned He now, lives to God.

Paul in his exhortation, moves from the experience of 'knowing' to the crucial experience of 'reckoning.' (V. 11) Knowing is a personal experience of the heart. A believer has to take it as a basis and reckon in his mind the ethical implications. He can now take into account that he died to sin and alive to God in Christ Jesus. Paul says that it must become his parallel experience with Jesus Christ. It is evident from his statements that 'dying to sin' means 'being freed from the mastery of sin'. Sin causes evil desires in the body. A believer who takes into account that he died to the mastery of sin over his mortal body, need not let sin reign in it. He can say that he is dead to sin meaning that he is dead to the mastery of sin as he is buried with Christ. He can also say that he is alive to God in Christ Jesus. There is a clear possibility to execute his option. So Paul asks the believers to keep themselves free from the masterly rule of sin.

From verse 13 onwards, Paul leads them into the final step in Christian conduct. It is yielding the members of the body. He asks them not to 'yield' the members of the body as instruments to sin but to offer them to God as instruments of righteousness. The righteousness of Jesus Christ which is deposited in a believer, is to be seen in his 'touch and feel' actions. Paul is pinpointing the freedom a believer has and is asking him to use it while exercising his option. Now, these members of the body are brought to life from death. This fact is to be 'known' in the heart. The implications are to be 'reckoned' in the mind. The will is to be exercised by not 'yielding' to sin. Sin is no longer the master. There is no need to obey. God is now the master. The members of the body need not be yielded to wickedness, instead they can be freely offered to righteousness. All this has become possible because of the grace of God which enables a believer to exercise this option. Paul says that the believer is not under the Law but under grace. Law imposes and sin makes man to violate. Grace enables. Man can exercise his option to uphold righteousness.

Contrasts the accruing results of the two slaveries (6:15 - 23)

When anyone comes to know that he is not under Law, the natural tendency is to feel free to violate it. Paul wants them to put a check to such a tendency. Once a person offers himself as a slave to someone, matter is settled, as it is done in obedience. He wants them to know that if a person offers himself as a slave to sin, it leads him to sin which in turn leads him to death. And if he offers himself as a slave to God, it leads him to righteousness.

29

Paul emphasizes here the climactic role of freedom. It is amazing to note that God honours freedom of man. Adam was free either to obey God's command or to disobey it. A man is free either to accept the Gospel or to reject it. Now, Paul is saying that it is only in this freedom, a person who is justified has offered himself as a slave to God. So there arises, no question of sinning. He makes a mention of the enabling role of the teaching a person receives. This man obeyed wholeheartedly the form of teaching, to the care of which he was entrusted. He is no longer a slave to sin. Paul says authoritatively that all believers have been set free from sin and have become slaves to righteousness.

Paul talks, now, about the down to earth practical consequences of sin and results of righteousness. He makes a mention of their past life to make them compare it with the present life, in its glory. He says that they used to offer the members of their body, in slavery to impurity and to ever – increasing wickedness. We see from this the nature of sin which can make them more and more wicked day by day. A person may not be as bad as his fellow man is but he has the tendency and potentiality to be fully bad. Paul's statement confirms the doctrine of total depravity. Paul tells them that they acted without check when they were slaves to sin. He wants to know from them, the benefit they got from those things. He is sure that they are ashamed of those now. He makes a categorical statement that all things they did then lead them to death. But God set them free from sin and they are now slaves to God. It is like a slave, after being set free, voluntarily offering himself to be a slave to the one who set him free. He considers that it is worth being a slave to Him who honours his freedom and did everything to set him free. The former life leads to shame. The latter life leads to holiness. While the former life results in death, the latter life results in eternal life. The wages of sin is death; but the gift of God is eternal life through Jesus Christ.

Shows the inability of Law to help in sanctification (7:1 - 25)

All his readers with different ethnic backgrounds in that cosmopolitan city are familiar with the marriage Law. He is employing interrogative sentences to impress upon them the fact of cessation of the authority of law on a dead man. Paul uses the analogy of a marriage relationship. As long as the husband is alive, a married woman is bound by her marriage vow. If she marries another man while her husband is still alive, she is called an adulteress. But she is set free from her marriage vow if her husband dies. She is not called an adulteress if she marries another man. Now this death of the spouse he applies to the believer. He takes his readers to the Law proper. He says that the Law ceases to exercise its authority on a believer who is dead in union with Christ. The believer by uniting himself with Jesus Christ in His death is set free from Law. Now he is united with Him who is raised from the dead. All the negative sentences of Paul, now, on Law are to be understood in the light of the powerful positive statements he made earlier. These are: through the Law we become conscious of sin; we do not nullify Law by faith but we uphold the Law. (3:20 ff, 31 ff)

Yet another contrast he brings in. He contrasts the new way of the Spirit with the old way of the written code. Paul identifies with them by calling them his brothers. Before being delivered, he says, they were controlled by the sinful nature. We can understand from this that this nature was the culprit in bringing the fruit of death. He makes another negative statement on Law. He says that Law aroused sinful passions and that they were at work in their bodies. These sinful passions bore fruit for death. He applies the analogy of the release from the marriage law of that widow to the believer who died with Christ. He says that he is released

31

from the Law. This release shifted the believer from the old way of written code to the new way of the Spirit. Now he is able to serve in the new way of the Spirit.

From verse 7 onwards we notice a definite progress in his thought about Christian life. At this stage of his exposition it is difficult to imagine that Paul is reverting to convey things about the life of an unregenerate person. Further his shift from 'they to you' and from 'you to we' and from 'we to I', is a definite march forward to present a critical phase in the journey of a believer, in faith life. His statements from fifth chapter onwards reflect the 'believer solidarity'. Now he shifts to individual life. He uses first person singular 'I'. Whether it is about, personally himself or about a believer, we are not sure. But it is the most crucial part of his doctrine. It shouldn't surprise us even if he were bringing his personal struggle to present a crucial step. Paul, in clear terms, personifies sin, very well clearing doubts about the negative role of Law. The struggle he presents in the Spiritual life of a believer is very realistic and applies to all ages and all situations. This struggle is only because he wants to please God on his own terms by fulfilling the Law, in spite of knowing that he is not justified by it. He wants to go under it in delusion, not knowing what God purposed in His grace, through the Spirit. Paul pinpoints the 10th commandment to unearth the motives and to expose the weakness of 'do's and don't's and rights and wrongs approach' in fulfilling the Law.

When Paul speaks about the sinful passions aroused by the Law, he is fully aware of the anger it would cause in his Jewish readers. So he anticipates their question: 'is the Law sin'? He vehemently answers: 'certainly not'. Then he goes on making series of positive comments on the role of Law: it is the Law which made him know what sin is; it is the Law which pointed to him that coveting was sin (V. 7 ff); the intention of the Law is to bring life (V. 10 ff); the Law is holy, and the commandment is holy, righteous and good (V. 12); the Law is spiritual (V. 14). He presents the evil role of sin by personifying it. We can very well understand his purpose in repeating his statements. It is to present with greater emphasis each time, yet making some progress in the thought process. He states that sin, seizing the opportunity afforded by the commandment, 'do not covet', produced in him every kind of covetous desire. (V. 8) In verse 10, while stating the role of sin, adds that it deceived him and through the commandment put him to death. (V. 11) This word 'death' in the context, is the reign of sin over a believer. So he says that it brought him back to the rein of sin over him.

In the thirteenth verse he questions them to know from them whether he was contradicting his own statement, that the Law is good. Does it become death to him? He says: 'by no means'. It produced death in him so that sin might be recognized and that it might become utterly sinful. Law is driving him to a climax. This he reveals from verse 14. Law is Spiritual and Paul admits that he is unspiritual and is sold as a slave to sin. This situation is evidently due to the undue love for the Law in the early stage in the journey towards maturity. He expresses his perplexity at the state of affairs, he is caught in. His intention is to do good. He is sincerely at it. He wants to see this happening. But it turns out to be the opposite. He does what he hates to do. He repeats it in the nineteenth verse adding that it happens again and again. Since he is wanting to do good, sincerely believing that the Law is good for him, he doesn't hesitate to say that the outcome is not his fault. He is able to see some other thing in operation in him. That is sin living in him. He explains it further. He says that he knows that nothing good lives in him i.e. in his flesh. He identifies the sinful nature in him with his flesh - the body, under the spell of the principle of sin.

Now he takes us into the thick of the battle enabling us to identify the two forces. One is his inner being who is delighting in God's Law and the other is the principle of sin operating in the members of his body. He calls the former as the Law of his mind and the latter as the Law of sin. The Law of his mind is nothing but mere delight in the Law. This delight is submitting to it when the Law of sin is waging a battle against it and making him a prisoner to it. This has caused him to cry in anguish for help calling himself, a wretched man. He expresses his utter disgust. (V. 24) In no time he offers thanks to God through Jesus Christ, the Lord for the revelation. He, now, knows the reason for Christian struggle. He sees the way open before him for Christian victory. He, now, knows that in his mind he is a slave to God's Law but in his sinful nature he is a slave to the Law of sin. So there are two Laws in operation in him simultaneously. When he says, 'it is no longer I myself who do it, but it is sin living in me', it expresses his unwillingness to line up with his sinful nature - the Law of sin. When he says 'I no longer live, but Christ lives in me', in Galatians, it expresses his willingness to line up with Christ - the Law of the Spirit. He upheld the second Law. This is integrity received in his person through a higher Law!

Calls for celebration of the life of victory and security in the Spirit. (8:1 - 39)

It is celebration time for a person who takes a positive step in line with the revelation he receives. Romans 8th chapter begins with no condemnation and ends with no separation. It leads us through the process of sanctification giving hope of future glory in the security cover of love. Those who do not live according to the sinful nature but live according to the Spirit are guilt free. They are set free from a life of failure, frustration and wretchedness and are ushered into a life of sonship, freedom, spontaneity, victory and security. Paul proclaims that it is through Jesus Christ that the Law of Spirit of life set him free from the Law of sin and death. There is a contrast between life under Law and life under Spirit. We can take them as two principles in operation in the life of a believer leaving him, option to choose between these two. One is the Law of sin and death and the other is the Law of Spirit of life in Christ Jesus. The choice of the latter is by the continuing attitude of faith in the completed work of God. God sent His Son truly as a man but without sin just as He created Adam without sin. He is the sin offering. So, flesh, the sinful nature in man is condemned. The Law was unable to set man free but God did it in His grace. Now, in the continuing attitude of faith the believer is able to receive the victory in his body by opting for the Law of Spirit of life in Christ Jesus and allowing it to subject the Law of sin and death to obedience.

The Spirit of Christ, who is the Spirit of God i.e. the Holy Spirit, indwells a believer. Paul categorically says that if any one does not have the Spirit of Christ does not belong to Him. (V. 9) The hallmark of a New Testament Christian is the indwelling of the Holy Spirit of that person. God says, "I will give you a new heart and put a new spirit in you; I will remove from you your heart of stone and give you a heart of flesh. And I will put my Spirit in you and move you to follow my decrees and be careful to keep my laws." (Eze. 36:26, 27) The Holy Spirit's presence in the believer is the only difference in the New Covenant. His help in following the decrees and keeping the Laws is of paramount importance in the life of a believer. Paul is asking the believer not only to be conscious of His presence but also to be aware of

His primary function. Christian character (fruit of the Spirit) is primary and Christian service (gifts of the Spirit) is secondary. Before Paul takes him to the basic reason for the possibility of Christian ethical victory in his mortal body, he puts before him the crucial role of his mind. If he wants to live according to his sinful nature, he sets his mind on the desires of the sinful nature. But if he wants to live according to the Spirit, he sets his mind on what the Spirit desires. Further, the mind that is set on the flesh is death. But the mind allowed to be controlled by the Spirit is life and peace. The mind that is set on the flesh is hostile to God. It does not submit to God's Law. It cannot, even if it wants to.

Then Paul states that those who offer themselves to be controlled by the flesh cannot please God. Paul admits that there is foothold for sin in the human body, though human body as such is not evil as Greek thought considers. Paul says, "But if Christ is in you, then even though your body is subject to death because of sin, the Spirit gives life because of righteousness. And if the Spirit of him who raised Jesus from the dead is living in you, he who raised Christ from the dead will also give life to your mortal bodies because of his Spirit who lives in you." (V. 10, 11) He tells the believer that the presence of Christ in him, makes a difference in him when compared to his past. He is having a body which is heading for death. But he also has his spirit which is alive. He is encouraging the believer to know that God will give even his mortal body, life, because His Spirit lives in him. The impossibility is now becoming a possibility. The ethical everyday life, which eluded a Christian under the Law is becoming a reality because he is opting to be under the Spirit. This is Christian life in all its glory!

The believer belongs to Christ. And Christ is in Him. The Spirit of Christ, who is called the Spirit of God is living in Him. He is led by the Spirit i.e., the Holy Spirit. The triune God's involvement is seen in the glorious Christian life contained in the eleventh verse. Having known all this, the believer should reject all thoughts about his obligation to the sinful nature of the flesh, since it will only end up in death of every element of charm and beauty in relationships of his life. But if he ruthlessly cuts away the misdeeds of the body, he lives this life of glory contained in verse eleven. Only such people are known as children of God. The Spirit is in operation in the believer moving him to action. Victory over sinful nature is not an automatic happening. All this, he can do because the Spirit he received is the Spirit of sonship - the enabling Spirit of the Son. There is no need to entertain doubts about continuation of this life of victory because this Spirit will not make him a slave again to fear. Paul says, 'by him we cry "Abba father"'. He emphasizes the togetherness in the family where God is the father of this one family. The closest word in English for the Aramaic word 'Abba' is daddy, an informal noun. It expresses the intimate relation of each one in the family with God the father. The cry could best be understood as a shout of victory. There is no fear of future.

Paul, for the first time presents the evidence of the presence of the Holy Spirit in a believer. The evidence is the witness of the Spirit with our spirit that we are children of God. (V. 16) He does not speak of any other evidence. It is to be taken note of by the Church, worldwide. Because it was only Paul, and no one else, who was inspired by the Holy Spirit to write in an orderly way the beginning and progress of Christian life. How does the Holy Spirit manifest Himself in a believer? It is only by giving him unshakeable assurance of the born again experience which can be equated with sonship. The manifestation is in his confession that he is a child of God and that Jesus is his Lord. (I Co. 12:3) This experience takes him forward to know that he is a heir of God, co-heir with Christ. It is because he shares in His sufferings, he shares in His glory.

Paul brushes aside the present suffering in the light of future glory we hope for. Sufferings surely relate to the sufferings Jesus foretold his disciples. He went through those. The disciples followed Him in that line. The believers should go through those because of His name. But we are destined for glory. This glory is to be revealed in us. The creation - animal life, plant life and everything on this earth – is cursed because of the sin of Adam. This old creation is destined for decay and destruction. So it hopes for deliverance from bondage and for sharing in the glorious freedom of God's children. For the present it is groaning. We have the first-fruits of the Spirit – His inward witness that we are God's children, His enabling work, His intercession on our behalf etc. While experiencing these, we still groan in the hope for the glorious bodies in the new heaven and new earth, the home of righteousness. Paul calls for patience in such hope. Paul says that the Spirit also groans while interceding for us. (V. 26) This is such a help we need to covet all along. Because, left to ourselves, we pray to God but we do not know how to pray and what to pray for. This is our weakness. Here comes the help. The Spirit knows fully well the will of God and He intercedes in accordance with it. God the father, when he searches the hearts of His children, fully knows the mind of the Spirit. Here is the perfect lining up of human spirit with God and His Spirit. Here lies the integrity of the believer in the present with a hope for future glory.

From verse 28 onwards Paul unfolds the grand plan of God in the life of a believer, which spans from eternity to eternity. The ground of his hope for future is God's love which encompasses all known and unknown things to a human heart. Verse 28 is the key verse. The rest is an elaboration of it. This is one of the most popular verses which a believer takes as a personal promise of blessing. Paul presents this verse to them, not to ask them to be optimistic in their suffering about their future but to ask them to enjoy God's provision in the present, visualizing the plan of God. A Christian is neither an optimist nor a pessimist. He takes things when God allows these to occur to him. Things do not work together for good by themselves, but in all things God works for the good of those who love Him. They are those who have been called according to His purpose. He proceeds to state the purpose in the following verse. It is to conform the believer to the likeness of His Son, so that His Son might be the firstborn among many brothers. Paul supposes that they all know this, as this is the natural consequence of adoption into God's family. It is to take as their own, the righteousness of His only begotten Son.

Verses 29 and 30 show the steps God has taken in that direction. Paul lists five – foreknowledge, predestination, calling, justification and glorification. God is omniscient, omnipresent and omnipotent. He has sovereign power. God has the power to carry out His purposes. Every believer consciously or unconsciously expresses this. He expresses this in his thanksgiving for himself and in his intercession for others. At the same time, he knows that God need not operate in a vacuum, as he himself can offer the members of his body, as instruments to exercise God's will. This is called human responsibility. Some monotheistic religions go to one extreme and say that God is sovereign and man is what He wills him to be. Some eastern religions, on the other hand, go to the other extreme and make man the ultimate authority to carry out his own purposes. But Christianity is a blending of God's sovereignty and human responsibility.

In the light of this, we have to understand God's foreknowledge and predestination. Foreknowledge is awareness of something before it happens or exists. It is God's attribute. Paul says that, He foreknew all those whom he predestined. While mentioning about the spiritual blessings of the Ephesians, Paul says, "For he chose us in him before the creation of the world to be holy and blameless in his sight. In love he predestined us for adoption to sonship through Jesus Christ, in accordance with his pleasure and will." (Eph. 1:4, 5) The difficulty we encounter here is with the word 'predestination'. It means that everything has been decided or planned in advance. How it is to be taken in the case of a person coming to God? Jesus says, "No one can come to me unless the Father who sent me draws them, and I will raise them up at the last day." (Jn. 6:44) St. Augustine in 4th century A.D strongly believed and taught the doctrine of predestination but he did not go to the extent of teaching that God predestined some to reject the Gospel. But in the middle ages Thomas Aquinas believed the doctrine of predestination, linking it with the permissive will of God to allow others to reject and incur judgement. During the days of reformation John Calvin believed it and taught it in the line of St. Augustine. It is true that God predestined some. If it is because of His foreknowledge, that they would eventually believe in the Gospel, His grace loses its value and man gains a point for boasting. If the doctrine of predestination rules out the freedom of choice, the Gospel loses its meaning. Those who teach it lose their urge to preach the Gospel in urgency. Predestination and human freedom are both Biblical. They are to be held together. Certainly it is a mystery. Believing that the secrets belong to God, we may take predestination, this way: this doctrine is for the celebration of the grace of God by the believer and it is not for projecting hypothetical theories on others. Paul doesn't encourage these. We truly believe that God chose us and predestined us, not primarily to send us to heaven but to transform us into the image and likeness of His

Son. We can say that the others only opted themselves to be categorized as reprobates. But who they are, we don't need to know or presume.

Paul uses the words, calling, justification and glorification as events which happened in time and space. God's calling to Himself, is closely linked to the doctrine of predestination. Those who teach effectual or efficacious calling take the words of Jesus as their strong basis. Jesus says, "This is why I told you that no one can come to me unless the Father has enabled them." (Jn. 6:65) The word 'effectual' or 'efficacious' means, 'producing an intended result'. Then the question arises: 'is it not a general call to everybody'? We see God's general call in Isaiah: "Turn to me and be saved, all you ends of the earth; for I am God, and there is no other." (Is. 45:22) Jesus invites all those who are weary and burdened: "Come to me, all you who are weary and burdened, and I will give you rest." (Mat. 11:28). He commands His disciples to go into all the world and preach the good news to all creation. (Mk. 16:15) Here again it is our privilege to celebrate His faithfulness in this effectual call in our lives and to believe, all the more, in preaching the Gospel to all. Our Job is to ensure that everyone receives the Gospel. Then no one can say that he is not called. Long time ago I was returning from college after work. A former student of the class I taught, greeted me. I stopped my bicycle and enquired from him to know when he would get married. He was startled at this and said, 'I gave you my wedding invitation personally last summer!' I felt ashamed. Why did I not remember? Perhaps, I turned down the invitation in my heart the very moment he invited me. Was I not invited? Yes, I was. Then why did I not remember? Because, I rejected it straightaway. Had I attended and witnessed the wedding and enjoyed the dinner, I would not have put such a silly question to him. Those who say they are not called by God, perhaps, come under this category!

Justification as we understand it now, is reception into the home. Glorification is participation in the splendour of God's presence. The entire process of struggle, a believer goes through and the step by step Christian victory he experiences can be categorized as sanctification. This comes between justification and glorification. Paul used the same tense for glorification along with foreknowledge, predestination, calling and justification. It is a matter of pleasant surprise to us. It is, 'past-future', a tense in his expression which is not unusual in the Bible. Paul says '... those He justified, He also glorified'. John in his epistle talks about this glory: "Dear friends, now we are children of God, and what we will be has not yet been made known. But we know that when Christ appears, we shall be like him, for we shall see him as he is." (1 Jn. 3:2) We are children of God. This is our present glory. This is given only as a foretaste.

What should be our response when we see this grand plan of God for each one of us?' Paul puts a series of questions to remind his readers of God's great love all along their journey. He makes us look all around ourselves to locate and to challenge the enemy who attempts to side-track us from this grand plan of God. God's grand plan for each one of us includes provision of all that is needed for us. Paul questions, "He who did not spare his own Son, but gave him up for us all - how will he not also, along with him, graciously give us all things?" (V. 32) Jesus had already promised, saying, "... seek first his kingdom and his righteousness, and all these things will be given to you as well." (Mat. 6:33) We have already received what it really matters for eternal life. God gave us His Son as a gift. This gift comes with a package. Besides this, When God is the one who justified us and Christ is the one who sits on the throne of Judgment on the Last day, there is none else who can condemn us. That settles the matter. Further, it is He who died and He who is raised to life. He is at the right hand of

God interceding for us. Paul goes on to list all terrible things in life to show and tell us that none of these can separate us from the love of Christ. He lists these, "Who shall separate us from the love of Christ? Shall trouble or hardship or persecution or famine or nakedness or danger or sword?" (V. 35) He says that we are more than conquerors through His love. Now He takes us to the height far above both benign and malign things in the creation to say that they cannot separate us from the love of God in Christ. He lists these higher level things: "For I am convinced that neither death nor life, neither angels nor demons, neither the present nor the future, nor any powers, neither height nor depth, nor anything else in all creation, will be able to separate us from the love of God that is in Christ Jesus our Lord." (Vs. 38, 39) This love is the security of a believer.

The Problem of Israel (9:1 - 11:36)

Upholds the sovereignty of God (9:1 - 29)

Paul takes up the issue of the problem of Israel after completing his doctrinal exposition. He is very well aware that the Jews will consider justification by faith as a stumbling block in their pursuit of their kingdom. The Messiah for them is the one who fulfils their dream. Paul calls this Messiah, the Son of God. He is none other than Jesus Christ, the stumbling stone God laid for them. At this stage, Paul wants the Jews to know that He is none other than God Himself - God the Son - The second person in the Holy Trinity. (V. 5) They are stumbling on Him. This causes great sorrow and unceasing anguish in his heart. They may not believe this. They think that he has gone to the other side and has become their enemy. Paul wants them to know that he cares for them and loves them so much. He says that he is speaking the truth and affirms that he is not lying. He says that he has examined his conscience in the presence of the Holy Spirit. It is a confirmation that everything he is saying is true. He chooses a form of expression to reveal his concern and love for them which Moses used for Israelites. Moses wanted God to blot out his name from His book in case He is unwilling to forgive the sin of Israel. (Ex. 32:32). Paul expresses his wish to be cursed and cut off from Christ for the sake of his brothers, his own race, the people of Israel. (V.3) We learn from this, the concern and love a believer should have for the people among whom he is born.

44

The people of Israel are his race and his brothers. He has high esteem for them. They are God's treasured possession out of all the nations of the earth. They are a kingdom of priests for Him and a holy nation. (Ex. 19:5, 6) Paul says that theirs is the adoption as sons and theirs is the divine glory. He knows that the fatherhood of God applies first to them. He also knows that they were invited into His presence which is His glory. Everything in true religion belongs to them. If we speak of a religion that God approves, it is only the Old Testament religion of the Jews. God made series of covenants with Abraham, Isaac, Jacob, Israelites and so on. He called Himself as God of Abraham, God of Isaac and God of Jacob. He gave the Law only to them. Moses calls it as wisdom, if they have it. God dictated to them every detail of how to house the Ark of the Covenant i.e. the tabernacle and every detail with regard to the sacrificial system in their worship. Nothing in their religion is manmade - their part is only to participate in the order. Paul talks about the highest point in their religion i.e. their relationship with God. It is the ancestry of the Messiah, the Christ. Luke traces His origin to David, the Patriarch and proceeds to trace Him to Abraham, the friend of God. Once Paul thinks about the Jewish ancestry of Christ, he is unable to contain himself. He says that this Christ is God overall and shouts aloud his praises in joy.

Once they are reminded of their glory, it is but natural that they wonder, why all this talk about their stumbling. Does it mean that God's word had failed? In this context, he brings in the topic of natural children and children of promise. While talking about circumcision he made it clear that a man is not a Jew if he is only one outwardly. Now he says that not all those who are descendants of Jacob are Israel and not all those who are descendants of Abraham are children of Abraham. To prove this he quotes Genesis 21 verse 12, where God tells Abraham that reckoning of his seed is not through Ismail but through Isaac. So children of promise only are regarded as children of Abraham. (V. 8) Now he takes his readers, who have already been startled, to a higher controversy of election and rejection. He comes, down the order from the sons of Abraham to the sons of Isaac - Esau and Jacob. He quotes from Malachi 1 verses 2 and 3 to prove that it is not by works but by Him who calls, things do happen. He brings in the topic of sovereign purposes of God and His election. Rebekah's twins were to be born and before they did good or bad God said that he had loved Jacob and hated Esau. Paul questions: 'what then shall we say? Is God unjust?' He answers: 'Not at all'. Here he upholds the sovereignty of God. God says, 'I will have mercy on whom I have mercy', while showing His glory to Moses (Ex. 33:19) and He asks Moses to tell pharaoh, 'I have raised you for this very purpose'. (Ex. 9:16) Basing on these two statements of God, Paul concludes that God has mercy on whom he wants to have mercy and hardens whom he wants to harden. This is indeed an outright statement on God's sovereignty.

There are those who want to escape responsibility under the cover of sovereignty of God. Paul anticipates their questions: 'then does God still blame us? For who resists his will?' Paul's counter questions make us understand what sovereignty of God in its essence is. They are: 'how dare you are to talk back to God? Do you not know that you are a created being? And there are some more to follow. In the limitations of anybody's imagination, the best analogy he can employ from the creation is the relationship of potter and the lump of clay. But God is transcendent – wholly the other. He is outside His creation. Potter and lump of clay only exist as His creation. The only difference between these two is of a degree. The potter is human and the clay is matter. God is the creator and the man questioning is a human being. So we can take this as his basic question: 'can the created being ask the creator why he made him like this?' Paul says that it is none of his business to question God if He chooses to prepare some for destruction and chooses to prepare some (showing the riches of His glory), for mercy. He says that the Jews and the Gentiles who are called belong to this second category. He speaks here as one who belongs to this group reflecting and rejoicing in the 'believer solidarity'.

Paul, continuing his emphasis on sovereignty of God, quotes two verses from Hosea and three from Isaiah (Hos. 2:23; 1:10 and Is. 10:22, 23; 1:9) to support his argument. All these verses relate to prophecies about the immediate future of Israel. Paul applies the verses in Hosea to the inclusion of Gentiles in God's plan of salvation. There are prophecies in the Bible which are fulfilled immediately. There are also prophecies which are fulfilled in the near future. And some more, which are to be fulfilled in the far off future (Day of Consummation). Peter also, as Paul does, applies the near future prophecies in Hosea to Gentiles in his day. (I Pe. 2:10) So, Gentiles who were not His people in the old covenant are now the objects of His mercy and are now called the 'sons of the living God'. The prophesies from Isaiah present a stark contrast. The Israelites, in their number, though they are to be like sand by the sea and stars in the sky, only the remnant will be saved. Paul says, that Jews (including him) would have become like Sodom and Gomorrah, if God had not spared the remnant. So whether they are called from Jews or from Gentiles, they are the objects of his mercy. This again, is a point for thankfulness to the Lord who is sovereign.

Fixes responsibility on the Israelites (9:30 - 10:21)

Paul reiterates his deep desire in his heart. It is that the Israelites might be saved. He wants to speak the truth in love. It is a paradox that the Gentiles who did not pursue righteousness, have obtained it. But Israel who pursued a Law of righteousness, has not attained it. The Gentiles obtained right standing before God by faith. Left to themselves, they wouldn't have ever dreamed about this privilege. The Jews could never have entertained such an idea about Gentiles. It is by the sheer power of the Gospel such a thing happened. Jesus while speaking about this said, "the kingdom of heaven has been forcefully advancing and forceful men lay hold of it." (Mt. 11:12) This has happened with regard to the Gentiles by the power of the Holy Spirit during Paul's days. But with regard to the Jews, Paul puts the entire blame on them for their fall. They pursued a Law of righteousness and have not attained it. In the Gospel language, the word 'attain' or 'achieve' is not a suitable word. It does not fit into the language of grace. The Jews thought that they would achieve. Paul says that their confidence was in their works. That is why they stumbled over the 'stumbling stone', Jesus. He quotes from Isaiah where God lays this stone. It causes men to stumble and fall. But the one who trusts in Him will never be put to shame. Such a happening was foreseen by Simeon. He said at the time of presentation of child Jesus in the temple: 'This child is destined to cause the falling and rising of many in Israel.' (Lk. 2:34) Paul has seen these days.

Paul says in the last part of verse 3 in chapter 10 that the Israelites did not submit to God's righteousness. This, he says is their fault. After fully upholding the sovereignty of God in verse 18 of chapter 9, he is now fixing the responsibility on them for their fall from grace. Is he contradicting his own statement now? It appears so. But the contradiction is only apparent. Sovereignty of God and human responsibility are both emphasized in the Bible. Paul is not presenting these as his ideas. They are thoroughly scriptural, though both appear to be working against each other. They submit to the mysterious purposes of God. Sovereignty of God is seen in hating Esau. But Esau's responsibility remained. He is blamed for selling his birth-right. Sovereignty of God is seen in hardening the heart of pharaoh. But pharaoh's responsibility remained. He had already been oppressing the Israelites. Jesus talks about the son of perdition, Judas: "The Son of man will go just as it is written about him. But woe to the man who betrays the Son of man! It would be better for him if he had not been born." (Mk. 14:21) What does it mean? It speaks of God's sovereignty and at the same time human responsibility. Judas cannot escape from the responsibility of his deed, saying that it was anyway destined. His deliberate choice is seen there. Why should Judas opt for doing it? God anyway would have accomplished His purposes. It is true that "the lord works out everything for his own ends – even the wicked for a day of disaster." (Pr. 16:4) But why should Judas or anybody volunteer to be categorized in the general list of 'the wicked'? Joseph says that his brothers intended to harm him but God intended it for good. We see both human responsibility and God's sovereignty here. Both are to be held in tension to uphold God's word. Extreme positions do injustice to the text Paul presented. We celebrate the mystery. Secrets belong to the Lord!

Human responsibility reaches its crucial climax at the time of considering the Gospel. The test of the proper use of human freedom is at the time of exercising their choice. Accepting Jesus Christ is only through faith. This is the only way to obtain righteousness. Here, the Israelites faltered. Paul says they are well meaning religious people. He is one among them. He doesn't disown them because of their failure. He can feel their heartbeat. He admits that they are zealous for God. What is the use of it, if it is wrongly directed? They framed details of their religiosity, by themselves. They felt free to tamper with ethical, social and religious Laws. Their religious rites increased with time. They did this all in the name of God. Paul says that this is not based on knowledge of His word. This led them to self-righteousness and hypocrisy which God hates the most. They were not submitting to God's righteousness. The one who gave the Law is the one who should give insight about the Law. He has come down to earth to give this insight. God made Christ central in the scheme of things. Christ has revealed God's intention with regard to the Law. He says that He has come down to fulfil but not to abolish. The one who fulfils is the one who can enable others to fulfil. Foreseeing the enabling grace, Moses says that, the one who goes in the way of God in fulfilling the Law will live. (V. 5) This is happening now. There cannot be a contradiction because the NT is the fulfilment of the OT and the OT is the foundation of the NT.

Christ has become available. The vain search for forgiveness with preconceived notions about the Law is to be put to an end. (V. 5, 6, 7) Obedience now has totally a new meaning. The call of Moses is now rightly understood. (Dt. 30:14) It is the word of faith which has come within the reach of everybody. It is the word the herald runs with, to proclaim it to the busy people. (Hab. 2:2) Paul knows the importance of knowing who we are, and doing what we should do. Christian religion is grace and Christian service is gratitude. Paul by His grace knows who he is and now in gratitude wants to proclaim this grace. He has come to the present and says that all those along with him who went through the experience of justification and who have been going through the experience of sanctification, now should proclaim this word of faith. Verse 9 is one of the four verses which are found in the Bible on how a person can be saved. It is: 'If you declare with your mouth, "Jesus is Lord," and believe in your heart that God raised him from the dead, you will be saved.' The other three are Mk. 16:16 f, Ac. 16:31 and verse 13. These verses give a clear direction for those who want to be saved. Belief and confession are integral parts of salvation. A person believes in Jesus Christ, who died as his representative and as his substitute. The same Jesus rose again as the first fruits of resurrection. This belief is the person's response to the conviction in his mind. By committing himself he experiences the result in his heart. A person who believes in his heart experiences justification and cannot abstain from confessing with his mouth that Jesus is Lord. This is salvation. Paul quotes Isaiah 28 verse 16 to express the faithfulness of God. Those who trust in Him will never be put to shame. The assurance of salvation naturally follows. (I Th. 2:13 and Ro. 8:16) God does not discriminate between a Jew and a Gentile while offering this blessing of salvation and the subsequent assurance. He is the Lord of all. He is available to all. Everyone who calls on the name of the Lord will be saved.

In verses 14 and 15, Paul expresses the indispensability and value of proclamation and the importance of the roles of all those involved in the missionary work. The Lord is nearby and is available to all those who call on Him. Paul puts series of questions to present the steps. The order is beautiful. It is a favourite portion in missionary conferences. Anyone can call on Him. But Paul's question is: 'how can they call without believing in him?' Call is to be preceded by belief otherwise call is of no meaning. There is meaning when they know about Him and believe. Faith is to be ultimately in the trustworthy character of Jesus. In a way, rational faith demands knowledge on the character of the person. This has to be presented in their hearing. So there is a need for the herald. God has committed the Gospel to the hands of men. We can understand that He does not want to communicate it through angels. These men are to be sent as missionaries down the order after the first Apostles. Paul quotes Isaiah 52 verse 7 on the beauty of the feet of these missionaries who go and proclaim the good news. He echoes Isaiah's admiration of such men.

When the good news is so simple, and when there is expectation that everyone should flock around the herald to grab the offer, why so few from the Israelites cared to receive? Paul quotes Isaiah 53 verse 1, where the prophet is bewildered at the response. Then he says, "Consequently, faith comes from hearing the message, and the message is heard through the word about Christ." (V. 17) This has happened in us. It should make us rejoice because God's purpose in preaching is fulfilled in us. Men hear many things. These are of no crucial consequence. But when the message of Christ is preached the real hearing takes place. And it generates faith. Thessalonian believers' faith is a good example of it. Paul says to them, "... we also thank God continually because, when you received the word of God, which you heard from us, you accepted it not as a human word, but as it actually is, the word of God, which is indeed at work in you who believe." (1 Th. 2:13) This works out in their life. But this wonderful outcome is not seen in the majority of Israelites. Then the doubt arises: 'Have they not heard?' They heard it very well. All Israel heard the news about Jesus. It began in Galilee and went around whole of Judea. (Ac. 10:37) Paul says that it is in line with what David wrote regarding the general revelation. (Ps. 19:4) Paul questions: 'did not Israel understand?' Is there any problem with their understanding? Paul quotes from Deuteronomy 32 verse 21. In fact, Gentiles are people of no understanding. But they received the Gospel. This happened according to the purpose of God. His purpose is to make the Israelites who are a nation to feel jealous about this happening. Paul's boldness in stating unsavoury words about Israel has a precedent. Isaiah did it hundreds of years ago. (Isa. 65:1, 2) God made Himself available to the Gentiles as though He was there to serve them. It is in spite of their not seeking after Him and asking Him. In the case of Israelites, God says that He has held out His hands all day long. But they stumbled over the 'stumbling stone'. They refuse to receive the good news. God calls them as disobedient and obstinate people.

Hopes for future salvation of all Israel (11:1 - 36)

After hearing, all that Paul is saying about Israel, the Gentiles may form an opinion that God rejected Israel. He puts a question to them to make them think about their attitude towards Israel and answers emphatically saying that it will never happen. General opinions may go wrong but the Scripture always remains true. Jews are His people. Paul knows what should have happened to him, a fanatical Jew, if such an opinion were to be true. God did not reject him. God foreknew him even before he was formed in his mother's womb. Even a prophet like Elijah was carried away by general opinions. He complained against his fellow Israelites to God saying, "Lord they have killed your prophets and torn down your altars; I'm the only one left, and they are trying to kill me." (I Ki. 19:10, 14). But God told him that he was wrong in his observation and calculation. It often happens to well-meaning ministers of God. God told him, "I have reserved for myself seven thousand who have not bowed the knee to Baal." (I Ki. 19:18) What an eye-opener to all those who are in frustration in their ministry! So, this event helps us to understand the concept of the remnant better. The remnant is chosen by grace. It is not by works! This is not to be forgotten. Others did not attain what they earnestly aimed at. Why? It is because they are hardened. Moses, saw that they were blind to see and deaf to hear. It was as though they were in an unconscious state. (Dt. 29:4) Isaiah prophesied that this would happen when the Gospel is preached. (Isa. 29:10) Paul picks up two verses from a Messianic psalm to confirm the state of affairs. (Ps. 69:22, 23)

Paul is developing his argument slowly but steadily to convince the Gentile believers that the fall of Israel majority is not beyond recovery. He is slowly unravelling the mystery, the grand plan of God. It is true that the Israelites transgressed. But because of their transgression salvation has come to the Gentiles. The story doesn't end here. There is a purpose behind this happening. It is to make the Israelites envious. Paul talks about his ministry in this context. (V. 13, 14) He is an Apostle to the Gentiles. He is out and out for preaching the good news to Gentiles. He has plans to preach in Rome. He hopes to be sent by them to Spain. He wants to reach out to people who have not yet heard the Gospel. But in the midst of it all, he has his heart's desire that all Israel might be saved. So he lines up himself with God for doing this. It is by arousing jealousy in Israelites. This happens when they notice God's grace to the Gentiles. He hopes to save some of them. In verses 15 and 16 we see his vision for them. He wants the Gentile believers also to have a view of what God can do to those other than the remnant. If their loss means riches to the Gentiles, their restoration in full will mean much more riches. If their rejection is reconciliation of the world, their acceptance would be an unbelievable miracle to the Gentile believers. So they too should long for such a happening along with Paul. This would result in unbelievable blessing to them. They should know that the entire dough is holy since the first fruits, the remnant is holy.

How God's dealing began with Israel, Paul wants the believers, to see. God made a covenant with Abraham. He reiterated it with Isaac and later with Jacob. It is holy. If the root is holy, the branches normally are holy. (V. 16 ff) He moves from here to the allegory of the fig tree and the process of grafting. He doesn't take up the usual method of grafting good shoots to the wild olives. There is no point in stretching the allegory to the rules of horticulture because his emphasis is on God's dealing with Gentiles, the wild olive branches. He sees that there is every possibility for the Gentile believers to become arrogant and boast over Israelites. The chosen people have been doing this all through the centuries unwarrantedly. He cautions them to be careful not to toe their line. They should fear God. His dealings with either of them are not to be taken for granted as His ways are inscrutable. They are a wild olive shoot grafted in and they share in the nourishing sap from the olive root. They might be tempted to boast. But they should know that the root is bearing them. They are not supporting the root. They may say that the original branches were broken off and they are grafted in. Paul wants them to know that if God did not spare the natural branches, He will not spare them either. He asks them to be always mindful of His sternness and kindness. He was stern to those who stumbled and kind to those who trusted in Him. But this kindness is not such that it would ignore leniency. This kindness is only to those who continue in it. Here Paul brings in a possibility which might reverse the happenings. If they do not continue in kindness they will be cut off. And if Jews do not persist in unbelief they will be grafted in. There is no need to entertain doubts about grafting in, the remaining Israelites. Those who are cut off earlier are natural branches of the cultivated olive tree. The Gentiles are grafted in contrary to nature. If that is so, is it not much easier to graft in those branches broken off earlier as they belong to their own olive tree? Paul wants them to know this, not only to be careful but also to join with him in his hope for all Israel to be saved.

The passage from verse 25 to 28 is the most crucial so far as the puzzle of sovereignty of God is concerned. Paul calls it a mystery. If it is taken as it is, no one would ever be able to blame God. And no one would ever be able to feel conceited. Paul's brothers in the Lord are to take note of it. Sovereignty of God and human responsibility are apparently irreconcilable. The blending of these two is a mystery and those who are in the Lord alone can accept it. They can also rejoice in it. Paul's presentation of it is thoroughly scriptural. He bases his hope on the New Testament hope, prophesied by Isaiah (Isa. 59:20, 21 and 27:9 f) God's covenant remains. God's gift and his call are irrevocable. He will blot their sins away. Paul wants the believers to know that Jews act as their enemies so far as Gospel is concerned. But as far as election is concerned they are to be loved because the Patriarchs belong to them. Now he brings out the positive cycle in which sovereignty of God and human responsibility interplay in the grand plan of God. The Gentiles were disobedient at one time but because of the disobedience of Israelites, they have now received mercy. If the disobedient Gentiles received mercy, the disobedient Israelites also will receive mercy. It is because God's mercy doesn't discriminate. He has His own way of doing things. Paul says that God has bound all men over to disobedience so that He may have mercy on them all. (V. 28)

The doctrine and its implications naturally lead a person to wonder about the riches of his grace and the wisdom and knowledge of God. The deeper the understanding the greater is the awe. We can very well imagine the praise of God's glory in the heart of Paul who has received His revelation. (V. 33 to 36) True theology leads to genuine doxology. He is sovereign. His judgments are just and no second thought should be entertained about it. His ways are inscrutable. Paul echoes the words of Isaiah where he compares the mind of sovereign Lord with that of men: 'whose thoughts does God want to give right judgment?' (Isa. 40:13) He quotes the words of the Lord who answered Job out of storm. Job says that he hasn't devoured the yield of the land of anybody without payment. (Job 31:39) In this context God questions him: "Who has a claim against me that I must pay? Everything under heaven belongs to me." (Job 41:11) God acts on His own. He is no man's debtor. On the other hand man is indebted to Him for all that he has received from Him. For, from Him and through Him and to Him are all things. Paul shouts in thankfulness and praise. He says, 'to Him be the glory for ever Amen.' (V. 36) We join him in saying, amen!

Practical Exhortations (12: 1 - 15:13)

Lists his expectations from dedicated lives (12:1 - 21)

It is Paul's usual practice to devote almost an equal section in his epistles for practical exhortations after the presentation of the doctrinal exposition. Theory and practice are complementary to each other. It is the being of a person that leads to his doing. What we are is expressed in what we do. Christian life naturally results in Christian service. Doctrine is the foundation and the practical life appears as its super structure. Paul after shouting aloud his thankfulness and praise of God for His inscrutable ways of grace and justice, in individual lives, turns to exhort the believers, on their practical everyday life. Christian service according to Paul results only out of gratitude for the grace we have received from the Lord. That is why he begins this section with 'therefore'. He taught them fairly enough on God's mercy. In view of it, he urges his fellow brothers in the Lord to offer their bodies as living sacrifices, holy and pleasing to God. This, he calls as their reasonable act of worship. (V. 1) If the principle of sin is made inoperative with the help of the principle of Spirit of life, body recovers its neutrality. Now, in all gratitude, this body can voluntarily be offered as a living sacrifice. In the Levitical sacrificial system, Aaron should slaughter the goat for the sin offering for the people. But here it is an offering of a believer to the Lord for service as though he would no longer belong to himself to fulfil his selfish desires. He is dead in Christ and is now alive in Him. This is a thank offering. This offering is holy and pleasing to God. This, on all counts, is reasonable. And this is the true worship. Because it is in Spirit and in truth – worship in Spirit with true understanding of Scripture. (Jn. 4:24)

Paul proceeds to talk about the practical implications of such worship in verse 2. Any detail in our everyday practical life should be according to the will of God. Satan and his agents - the flesh and the world - are waiting to trick us to sin. Though the principle of sin in the body is made inoperative, the world that is still under the spell of Satan has its own ways of conforming the believers to its pattern. It moulds the believers as a man moulds the hot raw glass according to his own design. But how can a believer escape from it? Paul has his answer: it is by renewing of his mind. Mind operates according to the prevailing value system. The prevailing value system is to be replaced. It can be done by the fresh water of God's word. God's word changes our scale of preference. Paul asks the Philippian believers to have the mind of Christ. It is the attitude of Christ Jesus who humbled Himself. Then believers will be able to test and approve what God's will is - His good, pleasing and perfect will. The renewed mind is the touch stone to know what His will is in our minute details of life. So we see from Paul's approach that knowing God's will is not the starting point. There is a process which begins by offering ourselves as a living sacrifice. Then renewing of the mind takes place through reading of God's word and obeying it. After this we resist the world and abstain from being conformed to its pattern. Then we will be able to test and approve what God's will is.

There is much teaching these days on God's will and many books are also being written to give various ways to find God's will. They challenge the believers to begin their faith journey by finding

God's will, as though it was to be the starting point. There is the danger of their becoming methodical and losing spontaneity in their spiritual life. Their dependence on God's word and the Holy Spirit may be hindered by occasional fervour. Jesus says that 'doers of God's will' (Mk. 3:35) are those 'who hear God's word and put it into practice.' (Lk. 8:21) Much of God's will is revealed to us in God's word by specific utterance and example. How wonderful it would be if we heed to His word and put it into practice! A few of the utterances are: it is not God's will that anyone should be lost (Mt. 18:14); Father's will is that all those who believe in the Son shall have eternal life (Jn. 6:39, 40); it is God's will for each one to be sanctified, keeping himself away from sexual immorality (1 Th. 5:18); each one to be filled with the Spirit instead of with wine; and singing, rejoicing and being thankful is the will of God (Eph. 5: 17-20) and so on. God's delight is not in making us search for His will in the dark. He is pleased to reveal it to us. His intention is to help us to fulfil His will. We have His revealed will in the Bible. We have no right to look for the will of God on a specific matter when we do not care for His revealed will.

Paul sees the believers as the body of Christ. Christ is the Head. He employs the analogy of the body to speak about the functions of the believers. There are different members in the body and all the members have different functions. Each member has a function of his own and he belongs to all other members. Paul says that there are different gifts of grace. (V. 6) The Spirit determines the gift to each member and gives it to him. (I Co. 12:11) In verse 6 when he says, 'we have different gifts', we notice that there is no hint as to when they received these gifts. It is a point for serious consideration. In chapter 5, verse 5, he says that God has given the Holy Spirit, but he does not say when they received Him. So we can take that Paul believes in instantaneous bestowal of God, all those necessary things when once a person is justified. So when a person is justified, events of great historical and Spiritual significance also take place along with it. Now the believers have not only the indwelling Spirit but also the gifts of the Spirit. These gifts are given with a purpose. These are for the common good. (I Co. 12:7) Through these gifts God's people will be prepared for the works of service. When they serve one another, the body of Christ will be built up. This keeps on happening until they reach unity in the faith and knowledge of the Son of God. This helps them to become mature to attain to the whole measure of the fullness of Christ. (Eph. 4:12, 13) These gifts can be categorized as gifts of utterance and gifts for practical service. Gifts for practical service can further be categorized as gifts of power, gifts of sympathy and gifts of administration.

Paul sees a very important point in exercising these gifts. (V. 3) There is every possibility for a member to be puffed up because of his gift. But there is also every possibility for a member to think of himself with sober judgment. This will happen only when a believer knows what happened to him when he put his faith in the Lord. Then he will be able to value properly His gifts of grace. Gifts are gifts of grace – charismata. Self-estimation is possible only when a believer knows what his Spiritual gift is. Humility is not refusing to know who you are. Jesus knows who He is and speaks it out uncompromisingly. His 'I am' statements are an evidence of this. Paul asks them not to think of themselves more highly than they ought to. That doesn't mean that they are to think of themselves less than they ought to. There are teachings and techniques available in the world for an orator to promote self-esteem in a person. But the teachings fail because they cannot offer this person a standard measure to measure himself and to measure others. Spiritual gifts give the believers an opportunity to see not only their gifts but also the gifts of others. When we see what others have which we do not have, however insignificant they may appear to the general public, we tend to respect them.

Paul gives a list of these. (Vs. 6-8) These are seven in number. In Corinthians first epistle chapter 12, he gives another list. In Ephesians, he gives yet another list. (Eph. 4:11) When the Scripture says that God has given these gifts to each one, there is no point in a believer wasting his time saying that he does not have one or that he does not know what it is. Every believer has a minimum of one gift. The sooner he realizes this the better it would be for him. He can prayerfully identify his gift or he can find it out from a mature fellow believer. It is usually revealed when he is busy helping in the fellowship. Since we belong to Him all the time, there is nothing like waste in God's time. Paul's words 'let him serve' mean that this person has license from God to serve. What a privilege it is! He is not saying, 'let him receive a call from God to be a minister'. So any member in the congregation can be in the service of the Lord. But this is to be in accordance with the gift he received. If every member of the Church is engaged according to his gift in the work as a labourer in His vineyard, how wonderful it would be! The members of the body function in unison. There would be total harmony. There would be unity. How good and pleasant it is when brothers live together in unity! (Ps. 133:1) Gift of Prophecy comes first in Paul's list here. But in Corinthians gift of Prophecy comes next in the order to gift of Apostleship. (I Co. 12:28) Apostles have a specific place in the early Church. It all began with the Apostles. They have a special place at a point of time in history. Now, in the sense of being sent, a member of a Church can call himself an Apostle and can function as an Apostle. But no one can claim the position of the first Apostles. Paul begins the list with Prophets. (V. 6) If it is the gift of prophecy, he can prophesy, but it is to be in proportion to his faith. The prophecy should agree with the established faith revealed in Scriptures. Prophesies in the Old Testament days were primarily for correction of the ways of Israelites. But this was by showing them what will happen in their immediate future. In the early Church Agabus, a Prophet, foretold the imprisonment of Paul. Paul knew it was prophecy to show what will happen to him in the immediate future, yet he gave more importance to fulfilling God's will. (Ac. 20:22, 23; 21:14) From this we understand that God's will is supreme. So the function of prophets these days, is to see that God's children obey God's will, by speaking authoritatively from God's word.

It is amazing to see Paul turning immediately to gifts of practical service, unlike in other epistles. Of course there is one exception i.e. teaching. It comes under gifts of utterance. Gifts of service appear to be so very ordinary - useful only in routine everyday life in a fellowship. These men appear ordinary. But they are also filled with the Spirit of God with skill and ability like Bezalel. (Ex. 31:3) Solomon has great praise for such men. (Pro 22:29) Because of their skill they do things in an effortless manner. Gifts of service can be applied to various fields of service. They often serve as a platform for exercising gifts of utterance. Teaching is a gift which comes under gifts of utterance. Paul knows the importance of this gift. All his epistles talk much about sound teaching. It is very essential in the context of false teaching which is on the increase. It appears that Paul sees God granting gift of teaching, along with the gift of pastoring, to some, as a combination with a purpose. Those who are supposed to care for the sheep and feed the sheep may need this gift also. Pastors are supposed to prepare well to feed the congregation with sound (healthy) doctrine. Further, teachers available in the congregation are indispensable for enabling the members to understand the Scriptures. (Neh. 8:7)

Gift of encouragement may take the form of public exhortation where those who are discouraged, lonely and depressed receive a word of encouragement. They are also like counsellors who become available not only to groups but also to individuals. Barnabas exercised this gift when he visited Paul and introduced him to the believers. (Ac. 9:26, 27) Contributing and showing mercy may go together and those who contribute are asked to contribute generously according to the needs. Their generosity is because of the provision of the Lord to them for this purpose. They are to remember this. The Lord's quality which was outstandingly seen in His actions was mercy. So the gift of showing mercy is very special. People are drawn to the Lord through their acts of mercy. It is very stressful as the needy constantly look to them. They need to be cheerful in doing these acts as the Lord did even putting aside food and rest. Those who are given the gift of leadership are to be diligent. They are to keep their conscience clear while providing leadership. The work of coordination is very difficult. Individual tasks of men have to be directed towards a unified goal. In leadership favouritism plays great havoc. The leader will have to keep himself away from discrimination in favour of or against some in the congregation.

Paul while writing to the Ephesian Church reminds them that they are saved by grace through faith. There is no ground for boasting as it is not by works. (Eph. 2:8, 9) He suddenly switches over to the first person plural and reveals something which unravels the place of Law and works in a believer's life. He says, "For we are God's handiwork, created in Christ Jesus to do good works, which God prepared in advance for us to do." (Eph. 2:10) We can understand the content like this. The Law did not save us but we are saved to fulfil the Law. Christ came not to abolish the Law but to fulfil it. Christ is the end of the Law. His resurrection gave it, its resurrected appearance - the righteousness of God.

It is the Christian Ethic to us. Paul from the 9th verse onwards shows how the Law appears in its resurrected form. It is faith expressing itself through love. The way he begins this section with love should remind us of the most excellent way which he showed to the Corinthians after listing the Spiritual gifts. He says that love must be sincere. Among these three – faith, hope and love – which remain, Paul says that the greatest is love. Paul wants this love to show itself in one to one relationship among the members in the congregation. When this is not seen in a believer, John says that there is every reason to doubt his love for God. Morality supplies us with principles concerning the difference between right and wrong. But Christian Ethic is our conduct which hates evil and clings to good. Paul calls for this conduct in our life. From this we understand that the doctrine of justification by faith which has become a reality in our life does not automatically yield Christian Ethic. We need to long for it and make it also a reality as we are God's workmanship created in Christ Jesus. Honouring one another above ourselves is not easy. The value we give to Spiritual gifts decides this attitude. Only when we are able to see the other person's gift and its worth, we honour that person as we do not possess that gift. Even if we possess it, the edification which we receive from him can make us honour him.

Members of the Church in Rome cannot afford to be lacking in zeal. They should always remind themselves of their central position in the world. Much depends on their Spiritual fervour. Heart is the seat of all emotions. They are to love the Lord not only with their spirit, mind and strength but also with their heart. They are to keep up their enthusiasm to serve the Lord. God was pleased with Phinehas and said, 'he was as zealous as I am for my honour among them.' (Nu. 25:11 ff) Paul wants the members to serve the Lord by 'fanning into flame the gift of the Lord'. (II

Ti. 1:6) Joy in hope, patience in afflictions, faithfulness in prayer and hospitality are to be exhibited in their daily life. Paul knows that they need all these not only for the present situation but also for the future uncertainties. Among fellow brothers no believer can live for himself. It is a family. They should be willing to share whatever they have with the needy. Paul loves this ministry and happily consented when the leaders of the Jerusalem council asked him and Barnabas, to keep this in mind in their Gentile ministry. (Gal. 2:10) Abraham showed hospitality to Angels. Priscilla and Aquila showed it to Paul. In the Acts of the Apostles, we see these qualities, particularly hospitality, in the homes. There is a concept called 'open home' which is very much necessary for the spread of the Gospel. Open homes are to be run carefully with discernment. Open homes accommodate travelling evangelists. They are necessary for pre evangelism. These homes offer love and friendship to neighbours and strangers. Open homes are also fertile grounds for training disciples. (Ac. 18:26)

Believers are to be amiable. They are to be available for one another in all situations. Solomon says that it is better to be with those who are mourning than with those who are rejoicing. In a situation where there are two families waiting for them, it is good to follow the advice of Solomon. Paul is asking them to rejoice with those who rejoice and mourn with those who mourn wherever they visit. He is saying that there should be willingness to associate with people of low position and willingness to do menial work. Harmonious relationship is not so easy to have. We need to make extra effort. Our pride comes in the way. We need to give in when our word is not taken. If we have conceit we fail in our interpersonal relationships. The devil tickles our ego. The greatest threat to Christianity is from within. He knows fully well that egotistic men can fight fierce battles in the Church among themselves. We need to remind ourselves that the same

Spirit lives in all the believers. We need to have love towards one another to overcome in-fighting.

From verse 17, Paul moves from relationships within the congregation to relationships of one with another outside. The Lord's interpersonal relationships are to be taken as a model. We need to commend a person when he deserves it; correct him when he does wrong. We should not show prejudice either in favour or against somebody, and learn to love the undeserving. There are people who persecute the followers of the Lord. Jesus foretold this. They do all kinds of evil things against them. Paul asks them not to curse them and not to pay evil for evil. On the other hand, they are to bless them. So far as their actions are concerned they are to be careful always to do what is right in the eyes of everybody. It is easy to say that the Lord knows what we are and that we don't bother about what others say of us. But the Lord grew in favour with men as well. (Lk. 2:52) Paul tells the Corinthians that he and his team are taking pains to do what is right, not only in the eyes of the Lord but also in the eyes of men. (II Co. 8:21) Paul asks them to live at peace with everyone as far as possible. (V. 18) There are everyday situations where people turn themselves to be our enemies. There need not be any reason for this. Peter writes about such situations at length in his first epistle. He says that it is better, if it is God's will, to suffer for doing good than for doing evil. (I Pe. 3:17) When the enemy harms us, the natural reaction would be to pay him back. Paul asks them not to be overcome by evil but to overcome evil. How is it to be done? Paul gives an answer by quoting verse 35 from Deuteronomy 32 and verses 21 and 22 from Proverbs 25. It is by leaving things to God as He is the Judge. We are not supposed to take revenge. It is his work to deal with those who harm His children. Our job instead is to feed our enemies when they are hungry and to give them drink when they are thirsty. This love will be overwhelming and they may not be able to bear it. If they react positively, we take it as His grace. God makes things possible. We can live at peace!

Now, talks about their duties (13:1 - 14)

The Church is in Rome, from where governance of the then known world used to take place. All civil laws are passed from here and the subjects are called to civic obedience, wherever they are. Members of the Church are no exception. Paul's advice to the Roman Church about civic obedience is very important. Paul has vast experience in this area during his first two missionary journeys across the world. Of course much more experience awaits him. His positive statements on governing authorities, at which ever level they are, reflect the early Roman administration known for its justice which gave peace to the subjects. The positive statements of Paul present ideal governance. These can be taken as the job description of a true and genuine governing authority. Church and state relations all along the Church history had taken interesting turns with changing situations and changing rulers. Paul's advice to the Roman Church has relevance for all times.

He says that every authority is established only by God. (V. 1ff) He has scriptural sanction for making such a startling statement. King Nebuchadnezzar heard a voice from heaven. The voice tells him: "... the most high is sovereign over the kingdoms of men and gives them to anyone He wishes." (Da. 4:31, 17) Other statements of Paul are: the rulers hold no terror for those who do right, but for those who do wrong; they commend those who do right. (V. 3) We know that those who are in authority are supposed to execute rules of morality. The judges in Israel are ordered by God through

Moses to convict the guilty and to set the innocent free and never to do it the other way round. Paul takes this as the administrative role of the governing authorities. The statement that a ruler is God's servant to do them good, is the most revealing statement to a believer in the society. (V. 4) The writer to the Hebrews says that the Lord sustains all things by his powerful word. (Heb. 1:3) There is yet another positive statement: the rulers give their full time to governing. So, all these statements of Paul are based on Scripture.

Hence, Paul instructs saying that every member should submit himself to the governing authorities. Since they are there because of God, he should not rebel against them. If he rebels, he is to take it that he is rebelling against God. So those who defy authority are deemed to be rebelling against God. (V. 2) Everyone wants to be free from fear of punishment. Because such fear leads to fear of men and in turn it leads to slavery to men. But who can be free from such fear? They are those who do what is right. They will be commended. The righteous man is courageous like a lion. The wrong doers irrespective of their spirituality, not only be afraid but also become punishable. Punishment is a deterrent to wrongdoing but Christian character is guided more by conscience. The believer is to submit more because of conscience than because of inevitable punishment. (V. 5) According to Paul when someone pays taxes it implies that he is submitting to the authority. We can infer this from the Lord's statement to Peter regarding taxes. Since believers are paying taxes, it is their duty to submit to authorities and also pay whatever they owe to others. These could be taxes to the state or revenue which should go to others' account. Paul says that the authorities deserve respect. He asks them to give due respect. Sometimes respect is only given because they are in authority. To some we feel like giving honour. They have earned this honour. So Paul tells them to honour such people. (V. 7)

Are there no exceptions to what we hear from Paul about governing authorities? It would be wonderful if believing members who are in authority exhibit such qualities. But we are talking about authorities in general. How are we to take the teaching of Paul when authorities are rude, arrogant and particularly unjust? Paul himself resisted when the magistrates in Philippi wanted to silently release Paul and Silas from imprisonment after unjustly punishing them. "... Paul said to the officers: 'They beat us publicly without a trial, even though we are Roman citizens, and threw us into prison. And now do they want to get rid of us quietly? No! Let them come themselves and escort us out.'" (Ac. 16:37) The magistrates were alarmed. They came to appease them and requested them to leave the city. This is a sufficient demonstration by Paul to make people know his mind with regard to deviations in rules. It was Paul's sit-in protest before Philippi prison. He is of such mental frame. We can never imagine him to be a compromising person. So, there is an exception with regard to unjust rulers and tyrants. Further, Paul never allows any compromise when an administrative rule comes between a believer and his God. He becomes furious. No compromise at any cost! His foundations are in the Scriptures. Shadrach, Meshach and Abednego refused to obey king Nebuchadnezzar when his decree came between them and their God. (Da. 3:16 -18) Daniel refused to obey the decree of king Darius, and did just as he had done before, with regard to his prayer and thanksgiving. (Da. 6:10) This principle applies to every situation where somebody, using his authority deliberately chooses to turn us away from God.

From 8th verse onwards, Paul, turns to neighbourliness and sober conduct. Paul's Christian Ethics often reflect the teaching of our Lord though concisely. Hypocrisy leads to false teaching. The Lord hates it most. Paul's teaching on it is in line with the Lord's teaching. Our Lord is not harsh on those who struggle in their moral life. Paul is also not harsh. Paul quotes the statements of our Lord on love with much enthusiasm. He asks believers not to let debt remain outstanding except as love – in the form of the continuing debt which they owe to one another. He speaks of fulfilling the Law here. 'Love one another as I have loved you', is the new commandment the Lord gave. It is the Law reappearing as Christian Ethic. God resurrected the Law as 'Christian Ethic' when He resurrected His Son. It gives every possibility for the believer to fulfil it. The one who has received the love of God, loves the Lord. God does not want actors (hypocrites) but He wants reactants, who love Him in response to His love. (Jn. 4:19, 10). The one who loves the Lord can love his neighbour as well. All the commandments beginning with the fifth one, through to the tenth, are summed up by our Lord in this one command, 'Love your neighbour as yourself'. Paul exhorts them to find the easy way of fulfilling the Law through love.

Paul's exhortation on sober conduct along with mild rebuke on yielding to sinful desires, is seen from verse 11. This passage is known for its effectiveness in the deliverance of St. Augustine. His struggle with the Law in spite of his faith ended dramatically in a park where he was called to read this portion. Paul's expression of salvation in futuristic terms here need not surprise his readers. This salvation is from the very presence of sin. The hour of total deliverance is at hand. All thoughts of gratifying sinful desires are to be put to rest. Paul exhorts the readers to wake up from their slumber. They need to put aside the deeds of darkness and put on the armour of light. They have to clothe themselves with Christ. It means putting on the new nature where decency is everyday lifestyle of a believer. Orgies, drunkenness, sexual immorality, debauchery, dissension and jealousy find no place in this new nature. They are to make such sober character their own through the help of the Lord.

Writes on tolerance among Christians (14:1 - 15:13)

Paul goes to a higher level in dealing with matters on faith. He begins this chapter by talking about people whose faith is weak. It is evident here that Paul is talking about the continuing attitude of faith in a believer that can be measured in degrees. On the basis of this grading, he is calling some weak and some, including him, strong. (V. 15:1) This line of separation can very easily be noticed in all Churches. Some of the members are categorized as weak in faith, not because they drifted into ethical failure in their moral life but because they are unable to reach the level of freedom God gave them. They are afraid that their actions may not come from faith. If it is true, and yet they do these, they fall into sin. (V. 14:23)

Paul talks of disputable matters. These are disputable matters because there is division on them. Some feel that they are not permitted by their faith to do a certain thing while there are some others who truly believe that they are permitted by their faith to do the same thing. One such disputable matter is eating meat. It is interesting to note that Paul sees both the groups accusing each other. The weak do not remain subdued. So this dispute is certainly at a higher level in the faith life of a believing community. How such convictions are formed in each group can be traced through further items of controversy raised by Paul. The group which is strong certainly is the group which has experienced the freedom, the Spirit gave them. Paul is the protagonist of such freedom of the Spirit. The other group is weak in faith. Who comprise this group? Meat, whether it is offered to idols or not by the butcher, before putting it for sale, is not a matter of botheration for Gentile believers that time. Considering some days special, can also be skipped by any Gentile believer because he is, now, no longer under the authority of his local deity. (V. 6) So the Gentile believers feel no religious restrictions in their new found faith. They naturally feel free in these matters and enjoy themselves by learning more about God from the Scriptures. Paul has known what freedom is and how Christ made it available to him. (Gal. 5:1) Along with Paul and the Gentile group there might have been a few Jewish believers who have experienced this freedom. We can presume that these are those who are called strong in faith by Paul. Once this group is identified there is no difficulty in identifying the other group. These could have been converted religious Jews who are able to agree with Paul in all matters of crucial importance. But there are certain things which they take as routine matters. These are: they cannot eat meat without making sure that it had not been offered to idols; they cannot treat all days alike - some are sacred days for them. They want to please God, all the more, in these matters. They are offended if other believers violate these. So Paul's teaching relates to Jew and Gentile division on certain matters. We may take his mention of these two groups, towards the end of this topic, as the basis for our presumption. (V. 15:8). We can also presume that he heard about these things happening in the Church in Rome through Aquila and Priscilla.

Paul identifies the tendencies of these groups. Those who are strong in faith naturally tend to look down on those who are weak. Those who are hesitant, without any need, and so considered weak, tend to condemn the others. Paul instructs first the strong in faith, to accept those who are weak, without passing judgment on disputable matters. He summons both and tells the strong not to look down on the weak brother and the weak not to condemn the strong brother. He gives the reason for not allowing them to do that. He says, "one man's faith allows him to eat everything, but another man, whose faith is weak, eats only vegetables." (V. 14:2) Another strong reason for not allowing either of them to react is the fact that God has accepted the other. (V. 14:3ff). Paul presents yet another reason. He argues, "who are you to judge someone else's servant? To his own master he stands or falls. And he will stand, for the Lord is able to make him stand." (V. 14:4) Attitudes like 'looking down on others', 'judging', 'condemning' etc. to correct the other person, will not help him. They leave him more frustrated. He refuses to take correction as there is no love in such communication.

Wavering faith makes a man unknowingly falter in his conduct. His walk is supposed to be not by sight, as that of others, but by faith. Hence it is necessary for him to be fully convinced before he takes a step forward. Paul, while speaking on this matter, is not bothered whether one is doing right or wrong. He is making known his personal convictions: 'As one who is in the Lord Jesus, I am fully convinced that no food is unclean in itself.' (V. 14:14 f) So if a believer is fully convinced to do a thing, whichever group he may belong to, and does it, it is from faith. Whether it is considering a day as special or refusing to eat meat, he does so to the Lord. While the other one who ignores these, also does it to the Lord. For whoever he is, he gives thanks to the Lord. (V. 14:6) According to Paul, all pass the test irrespective of two opposing positions they take in their action. So Paul's criterion for deciding whether it is right or wrong, is faith in which that person acted. Another reason why Paul allows each one to go his own way is, his position as the one who belongs to the Lord. Paul says, "For none of us lives for ourselves alone, and none of us dies for ourselves alone. If we live, we live for the Lord; and if we die, we die for the Lord. So, whether we live or die, we belong to the Lord." (Vs. 14:7, 8) In other words, Paul is saying that the Lord should be our very life and the decisions we make should only be in reference to Him. The Lord is Lord in all situations. To emphasize this point, Paul is saying that this exactly is the reason why Christ died and returned to life. He is now the Lord of both the dead and the living.

These are, Paul's words to the weaker brother: 'you who are trying to judge someone else's servant, look, don't you know that you and the person whom you are judging both stand before the same master?'; 'why do you judge your brother, then?' These are his words to the other brother: 'why do you look down on your brother, then?'; 'all of us will have to stand before God's judgment seat'. He quotes Isaiah 45 verse 23 in support of this statement. He is God. There is none other. He is asking all the people living everywhere to the ends of the earth to turn to Him to be saved. He is saying that before Him every knee will bow and every tongue will confess that He is Lord. So, all believing brothers, irrespective of the position they take in their faith, will have to stand before God's judgment seat to give an account of themselves. He is pleading with them, in the light of the imminent judgment, not to pass judgment on one another and not to put any stumbling block in his way. (V. 14:13)

Paul is taking them to a higher level of brotherly love. It is showing consideration to his brother. He is, now, taking them from negative attitude to neutral and from neutral to positive attitude. He brings in great Christian virtues – love, righteousness, joy and peace – in his arguments. No food is unclean in itself to Paul. And to the one who has experienced this liberation. But if anyone regards something as unclean, then for him it is unclean. The former is free to eat it. But he does not live for himself alone. He belongs to the Lord. So he should see how his brother is feeling about what he is eating. If his brother is distressed because of what he is eating, Paul wants him to know, that he is not acting in love. (V. 14:15 f) Paul proceeds by asking him not to destroy his brother. After all, Christ died not only for him but also for his brother. Both belong to the Lord. He brings out the repercussion of exercising his freedom. His brother considers his action as evil, because it is against what he believes, and he expresses it as evil. In the end, if the result, is one blaming the other, it is like making a very small thing too big a matter to reconcile one with the other. Paul makes a very strong statement to silence both of them. He says, "… the kingdom of God is not a matter of eating and drinking, but of righteousness, peace and joy in the Holy Spirit." (V.14:17) Righteousness, peace and joy are the hallmarks of the kingdom of God. All the members of this kingdom community should long for these blessings. They should make every effort for mutual edification. Such service is pleasing to God. Men approve it. It is growing in favour with both God and men. God delights in the expansion of His kingdom. Paul asks them not to destroy the work of God just for the sake of food. He points out the final effect of the act of the strong in faith in the fellowship. It is causing someone else to stumble. Paul says that it is an outright mistake. He condemns that act in view of the damage it is causing in the fellowship. (V. 14:20)

After making 'the strong' know that it is wrong, he is pleading with them not to eat meat or drink wine because it is resulting in the fall of their fellow brethren. He is telling them that it is better to abstain from such an act. This reminds us of the same advice Paul gave to the Corinthian Church with regard to food sacrificed to idols. (I Co. 8:12, 13) The last two verses in the fourteenth chapter reveal the possibility of both the groups drifting into sin. So, neither of the two groups should tempt the other. Instead, each should help the other to live a life of righteousness, joy and peace. Now the question is: how realistic is the possibility of their drifting into sin? Are the 'strong in faith' also susceptible to this sin? Paul says 'yes'. The 'strong in faith', enjoy themselves the freedom God gave them. Paul advises them to keep their freedom to themselves. Their belief on these matters is between themselves and God. Once others come into picture with regard to these matters, they have to be careful in exercising this freedom. Even on his faith in these matters, he will have to be careful. He cannot take things for granted. He will have to check whether what he approves is right in the sight of God. Paul says that he is blessed if he has no need to condemn himself by what he approves. (V. 14:22) So, there is every danger of presuming his faith and freedom which might turn to be otherwise.

Then, how realistic is the possibility of the 'weak in faith' drifting into sin? Paul says, 'there is every possibility.' He explains the matter this way: the man who has doubt is condemned if he eats, because his eating is not from faith; and everything that does not come from faith is sin. (V. 14:23) This sin is at a higher level in Christian faith. The believer sets for himself a rule to please God. It could be a religious practice which he thinks God will be pleased with. He tunes his conscience in this line. Just because he comes to know that another believer has done it, he takes courage to do it. This act is a violation of his own rule. It disturbs his conscience. Paul calls this act, sin. It makes him lose his freedom and spontaneity in his spiritual life. Paul's statement with regard to this is a universal statement which applies to all believers everywhere. It reads like this: everything that does not come from faith is sin. The one who caused this man to violate because of his act in freedom cannot escape and the one who took advantage of the other's action also cannot escape.

Paul identifying himself with the 'strong in faith', exhorts them: we, who are strong ought to bear with the failings of the weak and keep away from pleasing ourselves. (V. 15:1) The believers comprise the body of Christ. They need to build one another up. There is no other way in which the body can function. So the strong are to please their neighbours for good. They are there in the body not to please themselves. This applies to believers in all Churches, everywhere. What Christ fulfilled had already been prophesied. He did not please Himself. Whatever He did, it was only for others. All the insults intended for others fell on Him. He took everything on Himself. This is utter selflessness. Not pleasing themselves but pleasing their neighbours for good, is a lesson, Paul wants his readers to learn from their master. He reminds them that everything that was written in the past was written to teach them, so that through endurance and the encouragement of Scriptures they might have hope. His statement here gives comfort to all sincere seekers in all ages to learn from the Scriptures to lead their Spiritual lives. How often we wonder, whether things written for them those days, are of relevance to us or not! 'Are we supposed to apply these to our present situation?', is the question often we hear. Though Scriptures relate to things of the past, they are intended to be taken by us as well, as it is God's word for all. Paul sees the need of receiving endurance and encouragement from God. He prays that He would cause all believers to unite in one Spirit, while they follow Jesus Christ. He sees it as God's provision. His desire is to see that all of them with one heart and mouth glorify the God and Father of our Lord Jesus Christ. He bestows this blessing on them and hopes to see this happen. (Vs. 15:5, 6)

What all Christ did, Paul says, is much relevant to their situation where Jewish and Gentile believers co-exist in the Church. Irrespective of the proportion of their numbers, they are one body in Christ. They are to accept one another as Christ accepted them. Christ did this in order to bring praise to God. When He did this with God's praise in view, the believers are supposed to accept one another without differing on petty issues. On all essentials of faith, Paul allows no division of opinion. On non-essentials and all other petty matters, he asks them to give liberty to one another in love and charity. He says that Christ became a servant of the Jews to confirm the covenant of blessing God made with the Patriarchs. The second part of the covenant that all the nations will be blessed through the seed of Abraham was fulfilled through Christ. Paul quotes a number of verses – Ps. 69:9, II Sa. 22:50, Ps. 18:49, Dt. 32:43, Ps. 117:1 and Isa. 11:10 - to confirm Christ's opening the way for the nations i.e. Gentiles to share in the blessing of the Jews. So the deal is sealed. No petty differences can play havoc. The earlier both the groups learn to live for one another the better it would be for them so that they glorify God the father of the Lord Jesus Christ - in unity. Paul pronounces his blessing on them that God would fill them with joy and peace as they trust in Him. So that they are taken over by hope by the power of the Holy Spirit.

Conclusion (15:14 - 16:27)

Gives details of His service to God (15:14 - 22)

The detailed exposition and a long exhortation are over. Now we see the words of personal touch from Paul in these verses. He is able to have an idea of what kind of people the believers are in the Church in Rome. It appears that he has enough information about them from people like Aquila and Priscilla who came from Rome and made visits to Rome during Paul's ministry. He has many good words about the Church in Rome. He talks about their understanding and conduct. He says that he knows about them quite enough to say that they are full of goodness, complete in knowledge and competent to instruct one another. (V. 14) He sees the positive side of the Church though he knows that they need continuous teaching and preaching ministry, like any other Church. All Churches need constant reminding by the Apostles. Further they need to become mature in Christ. His epistle is not only for the present edification but also for keeping the deposit of his teaching for future, in view of the central place of the Church. He says that he has written boldly on some points. We are aware that his words appear harsh, particularly on Jewish Gentile division. They need to understand the grace of God in calling him to be a minister to the Gentiles so that they can appreciate his intentions. He says that he is entrusted with the duty of a priest to proclaim the Gospel to the Gentiles so that he might offer them as an offering acceptable to God, sanctified by the Holy Spirit. This ministry is entrusted to him by God. His job description and his performance are matters between him and his God. So far as we are concerned, we only know that Gentiles are to be presented by him as an offering to God - of their free will.

It is the only place where we hear of the personal reporting of Paul on his work. He gives a list of things that the Lord has accomplished through him. His ministry is leading the Gentiles to obey God. (V. 18) He uses the word power to describe it. The power in the word of God is seen everywhere when Paul preached it. We don't hear of any passive onlookers except in Athens. People either positively responded or created a turmoil. We see his deeds which are deeds of mercy as of his Lord. Whatever he said or did was through the power of the Spirit. Some might say that he is engrossed only in his doctrine. It appears so. For him what is first is first. Who a person is, first; what he does is next; being of a person to him is more important than his doing. Doing only follows. Christian life is primary; Christian service is secondary. Christian service naturally follows in a person who responds out of gratitude. The other way round i.e. service preceding life, will never work and it is a trick of Satan. What Paul does is to feed the Church with sound doctrine and then to challenge them to act according to it through the power of the Holy Spirit. Nowhere in the epistles we see so much teaching on the Holy Spirit and on the gifts of grace excepting in the epistles of Paul. If he is the only one who thought so much on the gifts of the Spirit, it is the duty of all those who emphasize on charismata to take his doctrine first. He says that his signs and miracles are an evidence of the power of the Holy Spirit. The signs did their job of projecting Christ. The Proconsul at Paphos was amazed at the teaching about the Lord and believed when Paul dealt with Elymas the sorcerer in the power of the Holy Spirit. (Ac. 13:12) The miracle Paul did at Lystra by making the crippled in his feet to jump is an evidence of his mercy. (Ac. 14:10) God did extraordinary miracles through Paul. Sicknesses were cured and evil spirits left people with the touch of handkerchiefs and aprons which were brought to them after he touched them. (Ac. 19: 11, 12) No wonder, the first Apostles were called, those who turned the world upside down!

We all know that he was a pioneering missionary. He says that it has always been his ambition to preach the Gospel where Christ was not known. Accordingly, his work began in Jerusalem when Barnabas took him there. Later through the missionary journeys his work covered various places up to Illyricum i.e. a place near Yugoslavia. He not only established Churches everywhere but also entrusted the members to the care of leaders. He asked all the members to exercise their gifts. So his ministry spread all over. So he says that he has fully proclaimed the Gospel in those areas. At this stage of his epistle, it is proper for him to make them know the nature of his work in the light of the ministry of several servants of God whom they have already known. He says that he made sure that he would not be building on someone else's foundation. He quotes chapter 52 verse 15 of Isaiah where the suffering servant makes the nations to see Him and marvel at Him. This prophesy, Paul says, is fulfilled through his ministry. The suffering servant, Christ, is presented through him in all these places. He was so engrossed in the work that he did not find time to visit the Church in Rome. He says that he tried several times to visit them but he was hindered by this pressing work of presenting Christ. (V. 22)

Reveals his future plans (15:23 - 33)

Paul does not want to be hindered anymore and he knows that there is not much work left. Further, his longing to see them and to have fellowship with them for mutual edification, is compelling him to make a visit soon. He has definite future plans. He intends to visit Spain and on his way to Spain he wants to enjoy their company for a while. He wants their prayer support. As a true follower of the Lord, his preparation for thousands of miles of travel - to Jerusalem and from there to Rome and from there to Spain and the return - is only by faith in God's provision. He wants to pass on the information about his plans to the Church in Rome. It is truly their privilege to pray and to participate in such ministry. The Churches even in these days should know to give priority to such participation.

There is presently a worldwide trend in Churches to give more attention to spending time, energy and money on administration and construction. The priorities are changing. This can be attributed to the absence of spiritual fervour and the lack of zeal on their part for the Gospel. In the name of rationality faith is being side-lined and social concerns are advocated to take priority over preaching of the Gospel. The world missionary conferences have changed their agenda since 1910. The earlier, the evangelical Churches realize this and change their direction, the better it would be. Christian countries are known for innovation and great scientific and economic advancement for centuries. It appears that some of these are slowly losing their position in recent decades. The decadence in family and social relationships in these countries is evident. It should become an eye-opener for remedial action.

Paul's evangelism includes social action also. Jesus said, 'as the father sent me so send I you.' We see Paul exactly as the one sent by Jesus. He undertakes the task of helping the poor saints in Jerusalem not as a project but as part of his everyday lifestyle. We see Paul's love for the poor in his teaching and exhortation.

He is now on the way to Jerusalem to help the poor among the saints suffering due to the famine. He has raised a contribution. The poor Church in Macedonia has given generously. Paul calls it as God's grace given to them. In giving they have known what God's grace is. Churches in Achaia have also been pleased to give such a contribution. Paul makes this a teaching point on Jewish and Gentile relationship. He says that these Churches, which are primarily Gentile, owe this contribution to the Jewish believers. The Spiritual blessings of Jews over flowed to the Gentiles through the covenant God made with Abraham and the Patriarchs. The blessings overflowed through the seed of Abraham, the Christ. In return for the Spiritual blessings, Paul says that the material blessings of Gentiles should be shared with the Jews. He says that this happened when they had given their contribution to the Jewish saints in Jerusalem. After making sure that they have received the fruit of his endeavour, Paul says, he will visit them on his way to Spain. He is sure he will go to them in the full measure of blessing of Christ. We know, now, that this turned out to be a great shock to the Church in Rome. But they might have understood soon that God's ways are different, but all the more effective, in terms of both Spiritual and material blessing. Paul went to Rome in chains, though as an under-trial person, on remand. These verses reveal the blessing: Ac. 28:16; II Ti. 1:16, 17; Ph. 1:13, 14; 4:22. Further, we can infer from Scripture that God enabled him to have some years of freedom before his second and final imprisonment, during which time his dream of preaching in Spain and also in other countries was fulfilled. (II Ti. 4:13, 20)

Here, he is, now, urging his brothers in the Lord, to stand by him in his struggle by their prayer to God. They have common bond with him in Christ and together with him have the love of the Spirit, to plead with God. He gives them a prayer list. First, they are to pray that God would rescue him from the hands of unbelievers in Judea. Secondly, that his service in Jerusalem, might be acceptable to the saints there. Thirdly, that he might come to them with joy only if it is the will of God. Fourthly, that together with him, all of them might be refreshed. It is clearly seen that he commits his visiting them to the will of God. How wonderful is the prayer request of this man of God! How pure the motives are of this servant of God! It would be wise if we take it from him and recast our Church and individual prayer lists. It is their privilege to receive from such a servant of God, the blessing. It reads: 'the God of peace be with you all!'

Greets them by name, cautions them and gives benediction (16:1 - 27)

Paul's strength as an Apostle is very much seen in his relationships. It is God's grace that he is able to keep so many acquaintances in the Lord in his heart. (Php. 1:7) It is the key to his success in his missionary journeys. At each place there were people waiting for him to receive him and at each place there were people in tears to bid him good bye. It was only in the hope of hearing from him and seeing him, on a future day. Besides this, these relationships played an important part in training his disciples, and trusting with them the care of the members of the Churches he planted. His interpersonal relations are also commendable. He always speaks the truth in love about each person, whether it is good or bad. With only a few exceptions the rest stayed with him till the end. Touring evangelists come into contact with many people. All these people expect them to remember them and pray for them. These evangelists need to depend on the Lord to be able to do this. Of course, these days, it is the pastors who need to take care of their congregation. Paul fulfilled both these functions. We find this extraordinary gift in Paul during his pioneering ministry in the then known world. When some Bible scholars see such a long list of names for greeting members in a Church which he never visited, no wonder, they entertain doubts. But when we consider name by name, it does not appear difficult for us to accept the list. There is a possibility of their contacts with Paul due to their frequent travels and the strong memory of Paul.

Paul greets every person by name excepting two who are related to the person greeted. He begins by introducing Phoebe to them. He calls her his sister. We see warmth in his relationship with her. He asks them to receive her as they receive any other important servant of the Lord. By this we understand that she is a minister (probably Deaconess) in the Church in Cenchrea. It is heartening to see that even in the early Church, Paul recognizes and encourages the gift in women and their ministry. He asks the Church in Rome to give her hospitality and help in her errand in that capital city. At her own place she is of great help to many people including Paul. She must have been quite an influential and important person with many resources. He begins his greetings by greeting Priscilla and Aquila. Paul presents them as an ideal couple. He calls them as his fellow workers. He remembers how they risked their life for him in Ephesus and mentions about it here with gratitude. This hospitable couple are known not only in places where they had to camp because of their difficulties due to their Jewish race, but also in all the Churches around. Paul says that along with him all other Churches of the Gentiles are also grateful to them. Further, they have a House Church. Paul greets also the members of this Church. The concept of a House Church helps ministers of God to take Christ to the people wherever they are. The organized Churches should not entertain prejudice against these House Churches. The present strength of the Church in China is in their House Churches. No amount of repressive legislation is able to check the growth of this ministry.

More than one thirds of the names are names of women. Paul's contextual statements on women to Timothy and to the Church in Corinth are unduly magnified and doctrines are prepared basing on these statements. How much place women find in Paul's understanding of ministry, we can infer from here. They appear to be crucial agents in the extension of God's kingdom. Paul says that Mary worked very hard for the Church in Rome. (V. 6) We can very easily imagine the kind of work she did in that Church, which is in formative stages. It is probable that Junias is a woman. It is amazing to hear about her ministry. She is a Jewish woman, related to Paul and senior to him in faith. She went to the extent of being imprisoned for the Gospel along with her husband! They were co-prisoners of Paul. He calls them as Apostles in the sense of missionaries. (V. 7) Trephena and Tryphosa appear to be twins and they are also listed along with Mary in their work for the Lord. A special mention is also made about the hard work of Persis, calling her his friend. (V. 12) Mother of Rufus, most probably wife of Simon of Cyrene who carried the cross of Jesus for some distance, is called by Paul as mother to him also. Julia and sister of Olypas are also women who are called as saints.

The good words Paul adds about each person while greeting them, speak the nature of his heart. He commends people when there is a reason. It is a good quality in interpersonal relationships. A fact about Epenetus – that he is the first convert to Christ in the province of Asia - is a matter of praise in the light of the courageous step he took. Paul says that he loves Ampliatus in the Lord. He calls Urbanus as his fellow worker which is not a small thing and calls Stachys as his dear friend. He certifies that Apelles as tested and approved in Christ. A quality which he asks later Timothy to possess. He says that Herodian is his relative. Being called a relative of Paul is certainly something special. There are those who are in the Lord in the household of Nascissus. He says that Rufus is chosen in the Lord. It is an evidence that Paul knows not only their names but also the work they have been engaged in. It is memory indeed! Greetings with meaning indeed!

From verse 17 onwards he moves to a matter of great importance and a matter to take note of with urgency. Paul speaks about it after his solid doctrinal exposition to them. Paul condemns with utmost severity false teaching as the Lord does. He calls it as gangrene which spreads in the body. The teaching, the Church in Rome received, is considered to be good by Paul. He is reinforcing it by his epistle to them. This is the touch stone to test every other teaching that comes their way. Paul urges his brothers in the Lord to be watchful of those who cause divisions and put obstacles in their way. They are there to present contrary teaching with a motive. In his epistle to Galatians, he dealt with such false teaching at length because he had seen it, taking root in the Church. Now, it is right time to caution this Church even before such a thing is introduced to them. They have to be watchful. Only when they fully know the sound doctrine they have, they will be able to detect the contrary things, the false teachers present.

Paul says that they deceive the minds of naive people by their smooth talk and flattery. These are tricky hindrances to turn them away from the true faith. They side-track the believers. They do not allow the believers to understand the Bible in its proper meaning. They distort the doctrines which are to be accepted in unity; they promote spurious doctrines. The pairs of truth presented in the Bible are not allowed to be held in balance. They ignore different kinds of experiences in the Biblical characters and emphasize only one at the expense of all others. They do not allow believers to tap various means of grace and make them cling to only one means. Full armour of God is not allowed to be put on and only one piece is shown to be sufficient to wage the battle. They leave the believers poverty stricken in their faith and defenceless in their battle with the enemy, Satan. Paul hopes that the believers would choose to stick to sound doctrine and his benediction is in that line. (V. 20) So, Paul asks them to identify the false teachers by their motives. He wants them to know first whether they are servants of Christ or servants of their own belly. Why do they say that they are in the Lord's service? Do they want to extend His kingdom? Pauls says: no! They have their own agenda. They want to build their kingdoms. They want to be at the centre of God's Kingdom while God wants Jesus to be at the centre of it. They want people to line up behind them. (Gal 4:17; II Ti. 2:17) They think that godliness is a means for financial gain. (I Ti. 6:5)

Paul tells the Church that everyone has heard about their obedience and because of that he says that he is full of joy over them. He echoes the Lord's words to give a piece of advice to them. (Mt. 10:17 ff) He asks them to be wise about what is good and innocent about what is evil. He gives his benediction after expressing the hope that the God of peace will soon crush Satan under their feet. It is: 'the grace of our Lord Jesus be with you.' Paul knows that the real enemy is Satan. He taught them to deal with the flesh and the world – his agents. Now, he makes them identify the true enemy. He knows that he is a defeated foe and it is only a matter of time that the believers possess the territory.

From verses 21 to 23, he lists his fellow workers in Christ, who he says, join him in sending their greetings. In all his epistles we notice that Paul's predominant language is language consisting of words 'we' and 'us'. It is the language of a true leader. It communicates his feelings of solidarity with the fellow workers and believers. He is so humble in spite of himself being head and shoulders above everyone around him. He lists the names of more familiar and less familiar people - Timothy, Lucius, Jason, Sosipater, Gaius, Erastus and Quartus. He permits, his scribe, Tertius to greet the readers by his hand. Some good words about the hospitality of Gaius communicate so much to his readers.

Finally, the one who asks them to offer themselves as a living sacrifice to God, is the one who is going to be poured out like a drink offering. (II Ti. 4:6) This drink offering is Paul himself, who is prepared by the Lord. This offering is holy and pleasing to God. Paul now, bursts out in praise and worship. His doxology is as follows: "Now to him who is able to establish you in accordance with my gospel, the message I proclaim about Jesus Christ, in keeping with the revelation of the mystery hidden for long ages past, but now revealed and made known through the prophetic writings by the command of the eternal God, so that all the Gentiles might come to the obedience that comes from faith — to the only wise God be glory forever through Jesus Christ! Amen." (Vs. 25, 26 & 27)